WINNING GOVERNMENT BUSINESS

Winning Government Business

THE **6 RULES** AND **9 ABSOLUTES**
FOR SMALL TO MEDIUM BUSINESSES

QUEENSLAND EDITION 2020

Thomas Pollock

Published by THINQ Learning
www.thinqlearning.com.au
government@thinqlearning.com.au

First published 2020

© 2020 Thomas Pollock

A catalogue record for this
book is available from the
National Library of Australia

NATIONAL
LIBRARY
OF AUSTRALIA

ISBN 978 0 6488021 0 5 (pbk)
ISBN 978 0 6488021 1 2 (ebk)

Edited by Martin Rusis
Designed and typeset by Helen Christie, Blue Wren Books
Illustrations by Zenzen, shutterstock.com
Printed in Australia

To my Grandmum, Patricia Higgins,

At least once every year since I was about 10, you'd tell me how much you were looking forward to reading my first book. I'd laugh it off and tell you that I'd get around to it one day, though deep-down doubting that day would ever come.

I always gave myself excuses as to why not. Too busy. Other priorities. Who'd read anything I wrote? Etc. Etc.

The one thing that always remained true was your unerring belief that I would actually get something to print one day. Well, Grandmum, here it is. This might not be the kind of book you expected, but I know it's going to help a lot of people and small businesses throughout Australia.

Thanks for everything, Grandmum.

CONTENTS

CONTENTS

"SUCCESS IS STUMBLING FROM
FAILURE TO FAILURE WITH **NO LOSS
OF ENTHUSIASM**."
—WINSTON CHURCHILL

Foreword

Kate Carnell AO,
Inaugural Australian Small Business
and Family Enterprise Ombudsman

THERE'S NO MAGIC FORMULA for securing a government contract.

It's hard work, time consuming, resource draining and, above all, lots of trial and error. Mistakes can be costly and frankly, many SMBs seeking government work have died trying.

But where there's risk, there's also the possibility of big rewards.

Some of those small businesses who have pursued their goals with steely determination have had success.

One such small business owner, Tom Pollock, has been there and done that. He's failed over and over, only to fail again. He picked himself up, dusted himself off and started learning from those failures, eventually winning his so-called 'unicorn'.

And here's the good news: by reading this book, you can learn from his mistakes, without necessarily having to make them yourself!

If you're a small business owner and confused about government procurement processes, this book is an excellent starting point.

The 6 Rules and 9 Absolutes is a straightforward guide with lots of good information for SMBs looking to win government work.

Tom generously shares his insights into the world of tendering for government contracts, including the stumbles he's made along the way and, most importantly, what worked for his small business.

A great lightbulb moment for Tom was realising his small business could partner with other small businesses to develop a consortium bid. This is just one of the many tips in this book that would be useful to SMBs who may have overlooked work because they thought they didn't exactly meet the criteria.

The lessons Tom has learned along the way and shared in this book are invaluable. One particular tip is so simple and crucial, but often misunderstood by small businesses. As Tom explains, often the government criteria are weighted by importance, which means small businesses needs to address these accordingly. As Tom learned — the hard way — there's no point in focusing on one aspect of the criteria that is worth only 10 percent while there are others that are worth 40 percent or more.

Another epiphany for Tom was when he accepted a debrief from a local council, following a rejection. At the time, Tom was angry and felt he'd been unfairly overlooked by the council. The debrief interview he reluctantly went to provided the very answers he was looking for. It became clear to him what mistakes he had made, and more importantly what he needed to do to improve.

A debrief is a really simple way for small business owners to educate themselves about the procurement process and what the winning bid had that they didn't. It's also a good way to get to know the very people in government who are making these decisions, which may make them stop and think about you the next time.

There's a Winston Churchill quote that sums up the message of this book perfectly: "Success is stumbling from failure to failure with no loss of enthusiasm."

Tom Pollock embodies this sentiment in his insightful and entertaining book *The 6 Rules and 9 Absolutes*.

There may be no magic formula for SMBs wanting to do business with government, but this book can certainly provide you with some of the secrets to success.

Kate Carnell

NEVER FORGET RULE NUMBER ONE.

The 6 Rules and 9 Absolutes

WHAT DO I MEAN BY RULES AND ABSOLUTES?

IN THIS BOOK, the 6 Rules serve as guides for how to approach, engage and ally with government. The 9 Absolutes, on the other hand, are some inarguable 'facts of life' based on my experiences about how government operates, including the main implication for small to medium businesses (SMBs).

However, there is an important distinction you must make, honoured reader; these are *my* Rules and Absolutes, honed through my experiences over many years. If you have anything from your experiences which you feel could help small businesses work with government, I'd be really happy to hear from you. In fact, anything that strengthens the small and medium business sector is of particular interest to me.

THE 6 RULES

SMBs that follow these 6 Rules will capture more opportunities to win new revenue through government work.

1   Partners must be actively sought and managed — always within a win:win framework.

2   Build relationships with and learn from peers who already work with government.

3   Follow the axiom that "mandatory doesn't always mean mandatory".

4   Prioritise criteria according to their weighting.

5   Stay the course. You will not succeed with your first attempt.

6   It all starts with a phone call.

THE 9 ABSOLUTES

1 Governments prefer SMBs with real-world cred. You need a private-sector track record.

2 The onus is on you to find government opportunities. Monitor government sites daily.

3 Governments will explain their decisions. Win or lose, always request a debrief.

4 Uncover the entire problem in order to position a complete solution.

5 Learn from the other side of the table. When government gives application advice, follow it.

6 Governments return to trusted partners. After you've won a contract, make it easy for government to re-engage you.

7 Position your resources where they'll have the greatest impact.

8 Modern Government Procurement and Payment policies have greatly improved. Understand that the historical barriers preventing many SMBs from bidding for government business are no longer what they once were.

9 Never forget Rule number one.

"SMBs THAT ARE ABLE TO POSITION THEIR BUSINESS TO ENTERTAIN AND FULFIL GOVERNMENT WORK WILL BE IN A **FAR STRONGER POSITION** TO NOT JUST NAVIGATE THROUGH DIFFICULT BUSINESS ENVIRONMENTS, BUT EVEN GROW THROUGHOUT THEM."

The biggest unicorn of them all

IN THE NEXT COUPLE of hundred pages, I'm going to share the wisdom it took me 15 years of trial and error to acquire.

You see, in my many years of good, bad, and everything-in-between business, I've seen meek and mighty companies try hundreds of different ways to tame the biggest unicorn of them all: a special kind of customer capable of turning around a struggling small business's fortunes, almost overnight.

I've seen them try books, social media, good-old ads in papers, industry-targeted campaigns, blogs, and promotional stunts.

I've seen them pay celebrities and influencers to throw their names at products and services they've never even used.

I've seen thousands of dollars stumped up for gilt-edged lead lists that are based on dodgy data.

I've seen marketing teams spend weeks putting together feel-good events that promise a tidal wave of leads and sales, but barely cause a ripple.

So many methods get thrown around.

Now, imagine me — perhaps just like you — politely waving my hand and freely acknowledging that I too have been seduced by the siren song of everything I just mentioned. And more.

Like you, I dreamt of floods of leads, opportunities and revenue.

I've sailed on all these rivers of promise — they rarely reach the ocean.

I've made mistakes that, even today, I still don't realise were mistakes. Other mistakes I have realised. Acutely. I've made mistakes so big and bad that, upon reflection, could be colloquially referred to as *alpha mistakes*.

And, every time I've considered the techniques mentioned, I've known there was a huge potential customer just around the corner. I've known that if I only knew the right people, or had the right framework, or could call on the right network, then I could find and claim my own personal 'biggest unicorn'.

When I talk about unicorns, I mean the type of customers most typical SMBs dream of. You probably know a lucky few SMBs that ride one occasionally. You also probably know that most of the time it's only big businesses that actually have a unicorn in the stable.

The unicorn I'm referring to here is our government. Whether it's the Australian Federal Government, the Queensland State Government or your local government (Note: several Queensland LGAs have annual operating budgets deep into the hundreds of millions of dollars), each has unicorns so big that they can redefine your entire business.

The good news for you is that I've spent much of the past 15 years working out how SMBs can increase their chances of winning large, reliable and regular government customers. That is to say, of riding the biggest unicorn of them all.

This book is about everything I've learned. As you'll soon understand, there are no miracle lead lists, no advice on expensive marketing campaigns, no tips for holding a flashy event, no insider knowledge on celebrity endorsements and no how-to guide for hiring ex-government heavyweights. Why? Because this book is about what works.

The secret you're about to find out is that the ways to claim your 'biggest unicorn' are simpler ... and smarter. Before I can share everything I've learned, I have to tell you some of my story ...

THE JOURNEY BEGINS

In 1999, I left my home and came to the big city. I began earning my stripes as a humble account executive for a company specialising in educational services. Starting at the ground level, I focused on the small to medium corporate Business to Business (B2B) market. Over the next couple of years, I earned further stripes and won a promotion. I was essentially performing the same role, only now for larger national companies. In 2003, I was promoted again and asked to manage an underperforming location. My mission was to make it profitable.

So I did.

My location grew considerably and our team began to make a name for itself offering services that our local market valued and respected. Of course, with growth came more responsibility. Soon, we had to hire more staff. So, I was now managing more people. I was also establishing valuable partner alliances, maintaining operations and coaching staff on things I thought only I knew or which I believed I did best. I had my nose in everything. To stay on top of it all, I often worked ridiculously long hours. Weekends, ha!

Then, one day, I had my first awakening: this situation sucked and I wanted out.

Unfortunately, there was no quick and easy way to regain my lost balance. Nevertheless, something had to change. My social life was dead from neglect. My wife would, at some point, get the shits with only having a part-time husband. I could imagine my three sons growing up to disown me because I'd missed all of their special moments.

I looked at what I thought I hated in my job. I looked at what was taking up most of my time. I looked at what I missed most from my halcyon days with the company.

EUREKA! PART I

After much reflection, I realised there was nothing I truly *hated* in my job, but there were two salient factors to my disaffection. First, there was too much taking up my time. Second, I determined that something was missing from my glory/happy/run-into-work-skipping-with-a-bluebird-on-my-shoulder days. I soon realised that both 'deal-breakers' were one and the same ...

I realised that what I missed most was talking to customers directly, putting together solutions for them and then presenting them in person. Yet, as is often the way with increasing management responsibility, my role had become less and less client facing. I had devolved into dealing almost entirely with the company's internal issues, problematic situations and meetings-meetings-meetings. Did I mention all the meetings?

Upon realising what was going wrong, I worked on a plan and presented it to head office. If I could delegate half my current duties to others, I could then use my new 'free time' to service customers directly.

Surprisingly, my proposal was accepted. Next, I needed to determine which industry vertical or clients I would actually look after moving forward. This was important: I didn't want our sales team to lose any of their existing clients due to me 'taking over'. I'd witnessed first-hand that this would end in tears, resignations and a damaged culture.

Thus, in searching for the right vertical, I specifically looked into sectors that:

a. We weren't already embedded in. Nothing ticked this box.
b. We were doing a minor amount of business in, but which had far more potential. A few sectors ticked this,

but chasing them would still mean taking clients away from our BDMs.

c. Had the potential to significantly boost the company's bottom line.

Sadly, nothing immediately grabbed me with claims to satisfy points a, b and c.

EUREKA! PART II

One seemingly normal day, the front desk buzzed asking me to take a call from a potential customer. A person from a state government department was waiting on the line. We'd had calls like this before and I knew how it was going to go: they'd make an enquiry, then vanish despite all efforts to engage them.

See, the company I worked for had already made scores of attempts to get any level of government to take on our services. We'd spent not hours, not days, but *weeks* putting together responses for government that seemed perfectly suited to our offering. Nothing worked.

We'd called many different government areas, and we'd chased any and all scraps of business as usual (BAU) work. No real success there either.

We'd sent proposals, quotes, special government promotions (which weren't really that special in hindsight) ... you name it, we'd tried it. None of it worked. Compounding all this, we weren't on any government panels, we had no government story and we had no-one in the business who had experience (read: good experience) working with any level of government.

Lastly, we had a big national competitor that was already deeply embedded in government. We knew they were sitting at the table supping on lucrative contracts and likely doing everything they could to ensure no-one else would get an invitation to dinner.

To be fair, we had scored a single lucky break within a small area of one large department, but that was a slice of the pie so thin you could have seen through it. And, make no mistake, the government pie is so big that even small slices can anchor entire businesses. However, our single 'lucky slice' was still so vanishingly thin it didn't even cover morning tea.

So, we felt like we were bashing our heads against a government brick wall that wasn't going to give way any time soon. As happens sometimes, we almost subliminally decided government work wasn't for us. We all but stopped hunting for that unicorn.

And now, I had someone from the government waiting on hold for what I thought was to be another morale-sapping spin on the empty enquiry merry-go-round. Of course, I took the call, but I didn't expect much.

A training officer from a smaller government department was waiting on the line. He'd noticed we had a course running in two weeks and asked if we had space for three extra people. I said "sure". I emailed him a registration form and put it out of my mind, believing it to be just another of what I call "we just needed a third quote and have no real desire to utilise your services" lead.

Then, just 30 minutes later, my email alert sounded its call. I opened the attachment and there it was. A signed registration form from the training officer's department worth $10,900! Even more astonishing, directly beneath were credit card details and the authorising person's name, direct number and title.

Praise be! The lightbulb had finally switched on. The apple had dropped and thudded soundly on my head. The problem was solved. I knew what would become 'my sector'.

I would specialise in securing government business. And so I got to work.

STUMBLING UP THE MOUNTAIN

I spent the next three years knocking on government doors. Some opened. Most didn't. I'm pretty stubborn. I kept knocking, and learning, and knocking, and learning. Over time I began to understand what government was looking for from its suppliers. Over time I began to understand how to put myself in a position to work with government. Over time I began to position our company in a much stronger place to secure government business.

Over the next three years, more government work came our way. I kept learning. At the same time I was growing a strong network of government officials who'd at least take my calls — sometimes.

Over the next few years, government work came to account for 18 percent of our company's revenue. It had become the regular purchaser that I'd always hoped it would be if I ever figured out how to reach it. Importantly, our government business had two qualities that private sector work often lacked: as an SMB, we craved customers that provided regular and reliable work. And now, after a pretty long time and a lot of work, my company had a new reliable revenue stream that would only grow over time. It was around this time that I began to understand that government work wasn't just any unicorn, it was the biggest unicorn of them all!

THE 6 RULES AND 9 ABSOLUTES

In tough economic times — and this country is moving into some choppy waters — government is one of the few sectors that continues to spend. In fact, during troubled economic periods governments are almost guaranteed to increase their spending in a bid to prevent an economic crash.

SMBs that are able to position their business to entertain and fulfil government work will be in a far stronger position to not just navigate though difficult business environments, but even grow throughout them.

This book is about how to ride the biggest unicorn and reach a market that you either haven't considered or that you've put into the too-hard basket.

I can't and won't guarantee that you'll be swimming in government work — that's not what this book is designed to do. Rather, this book is something of a journal outlining everything I've learned in the past 15 years of working with government.

This book will help SMBs level the playing field and help them compete against much bigger companies when it comes to securing government business. The principles are the same and the techniques work whether you're chasing $1000 or $1,000,000. And, perhaps most importantly, this book arms SMBs with better insight and a greater understanding of what government is searching for when it looks to partner with the private sector.

If you really buy in to this government journey, your business will, by the end, be in a strong position to bid for public-sector business. Getting there means learning the 6 Rules and 9 Absolutes of partnering with government. On these 15 imperatives and commandments you can hang a plan for evolving your SMB into something 'government ready'.

Consistently apply the 6 and the 9 and you can:
- Bid for government work with confidence
- Increase your chances of winning government work
- Drive down the engagement risk you present to government
- Watch your SMB become an attractive and trustworthy potential government supplier.

If you'd like to know more about the 6 Rules and 9 Absolutes, then let's begin.

"WHEN WORKING WITH GOVERNMENT, KNOWLEDGE ISN'T POWER. **UNDERSTANDING IS POWER**. WHEN WE FIND A SUPPLIER WHO UNDERSTANDS HOW WE WORK, UNDERSTANDS OUR PROBLEMS AND CHALLENGES AND UNDERSTANDS WHAT WE WANT, THEN WE KNOW WE HAVE A COMPANY THAT WE CAN CONFIDENTLY PARTNER WITH."

CHAPTER ONE

Knowledge is *understanding,* not power

WHEN I STARTED PURSUING government work, for a long time it felt like I was trying to break in a pair of shoes that was a size too small.

I was uncomfortable most of the time. I got 'blisters' as I poked and prodded into different government departments with little-to-no meaningful outcomes. After some time, this fruitless pursuit meant my morale developed a limp.

In those days I had a massive stubborn streak, so I pushed through. I was committed to breaking in my government shoes and decided it might go faster if I got smarter about it. I realised there were four things I didn't know enough about:

1. A map of the different government departments
2. Their function
3. Departmental goals and strategic objectives
4. Key personnel within the relevant departments.

THE KEY

I've worked with a lot of government officials over the years. Many have generously given me their time for phone calls, emails and meetings. They've helped me learn more about them, their departments, their challenges and their strategic goals. They've helped me navigate the twists and turns of working with government. Without them, I wouldn't have achieved much at all in the government sector.

One day I was sitting down with a distinguished senior government official and he said something that really resonated with me, and not just because it served to grow my Government IQ. During this meeting I had been explaining how I knew our company could help a certain department but that our approaches were coming up short because we didn't know enough about their needs to position ourselves as a solution's provider.

"Knowledge is power," I concluded with a shrug.

The official shook his head ever-so-slightly and corrected me:

"When working with government, knowledge isn't power. Understanding is power. When we find a supplier who understands how we work, understands our problems and challenges and understands what we want, then we know we have a company that we can confidently partner with."

GROW YOUR GOVERNMENT IQ

If you, as an SMB, decide to devote time and energy to attracting government work, then you'll need to increase your knowledge and understanding of the area, or areas, within government that you're targeting. Here's a non-comprehensive list of questions you need thorough answers to:

- What exactly do they do?
- How many staff do they have?
- Any chance of an organisation chart?
- What projects do they have on?
- What projects have been completed?
- What are their objectives over the next 12 months?
- How do they make purchasing decisions?
- How do they plan to meet their departmental goals?

Start, but don't stop, with Google

You might have to think laterally to get the answers; you might just have to get Googling. In fact, Google is a great place to start because government departments publish a lot of information about themselves.

Want to know the names of some business managers with the Department of Whatever? Google it and you'll likely get some answers from the departmental site, LinkedIn or some other web source.

Want to find out which departments are planning projects around digital transformation? Google it: you might be surprised at how much information is publicly available.

Beware: just because it's on Google, doesn't mean it's true. The search results you find must be validated.

Subscribe, subscribe, subscribe

After you've done your first round of Googling, you're ready to subscribe to the newsletters that many government departments produce. When you do, you automatically tap into an information feed that reveals what said department is doing and planning to do.

These newsletters aren't the pot of government gold at the end of the rainbow, but they will increase your knowledge of different government departments. I've noted a few examples for you at the end of this section.

Talk to the people

Googling and newsletter subscriptions are simple and you can do this immediately, the next — and the most powerful — way to grow your government IQ is to talk to the people who are in the thick of it. You'll soon gain real insights into government areas. Like a kid offered a cupcake, you must grasp every opportunity to speak to and network with government staff. Pretty quickly your government IQ will grow. You'll uncover many interesting things — like what projects are challenging, what new initiatives are being discussed and who has been recently appointed and where.

This will all help to reinforce your government IQ in many ways. Here are just a few:

- You will have more meaningful conversations with government decision makers (DMs).
- You can demonstrate to DMs that you understand their department far deeper than many of their current and prospective suppliers.
- You will differentiate yourself from other suppliers in your industry.
- You'll have the knowledge to offer insights into up-coming projects and expected challenges.

Spending 20 to 30 minutes every few days going over government communications might sound boring ... well, it is! Painfully so.

However, the first time you apply your learnings when talking to a real government employee in the real world, I want you to carefully watch how they respond. And, I'm not just referring to what they say. More so, I want you to see how their body language changes as they relax a bit more and engage with you on a deeper level.

They will begin to see you as someone who might offer them far more value in the future.

They will begin to see you as someone who understands their department and its upcoming challenges.

They will begin to see you as different from most other suppliers.

And, perhaps most importantly, they'll remember you.

Don't know where to start? Here are a few online places where you can sign up for government comms — it is by no means exhaustive!

WORTHWHILE GOVERNMENT INFORMATION FEEDS

Department of Local Government, Racing and Multicultural affairs
Go to: About Us > News, media and events > Local Government Bulletins
URL: https://www.dlgrma.qld.gov.au/about-ilgp/news-media-and-events/local-government-bulletins.html

State Development, Manufacturing, Infrastructure and Planning
Go to: News > Sharing our stories > Keep up to date
URL: https://www.dsdmip.qld.gov.au/news-and-events/sharing-our-stories/keep-up-to-date.html

Queensland Audit Office
Go to: Reports and resources > Scroll to the bottom of the page > Input your details at "Subscribe to our news and blog"
URL: https://www.qao.qld.gov.au/reports-resources

Moreton Bay Regional Council
Go to: News on the bottom of the page > Newsletters > Subscribe
URL: https://www.moretonbay.qld.gov.au/News/Newsletters

Department of Housing and Public Works
Go to: About us > Reports and publications > Newsletters
URL: https://www.hpw.qld.gov.au/aboutus/ReportsPublications/Newsletters/Pages/default.aspx

City of Ipswich
Go to: Media releases at top of page > Newsletters link on right of page
URL: https://www.ipswich.qld.gov.au/about_council/media/newsletters

Queensland Health
Go to: News & events > Newsletter
URL: https://www.health.qld.gov.au/news-events/newsletter

Advance Queensland
Go to: Scroll to the bottom of the page > Click the newspaper icon

URL: https://advance.qld.gov.au/advance-queensland-enewsletter

Business Queensland "Inside Liquor and Gaming newsletter"
Go to: Hospitality, tourism and sport > Liquor and gaming > Inside Liquor and Gaming newsletter

URL: https://www.business.qld.gov.au/industries/hospitality-tourism-sport/liquor-gaming/liquor/newsletter

Queensland Ombudsman
Go to: Improve public administration > Newsletters

URL: https://www.ombudsman.qld.gov.au/improve-public-administration/newsletters

Fair trading newsletters
Go to: For Queenslanders > Your rights, crime and the law
> Laws, regulated industries and accountability
> Queensland laws and regulations
> Fair trading services, programs and resources
> Fair trading newsletters

URL: https://www.qld.gov.au/law/laws-regulated-industries-and-accountability/queensland-laws-and-regulations/fair-trading-services-programs-and-resources/fair-trading-newsletters

Department of Local Government, Racing and Multicultural Affairs news
Go to: Department of Local Government, Racing and Multicultural Affairs homepage > About us > News, media and events > Subscribe

URL: http://www.dlgrma.qld.gov.au/about-ilgp/news-media-and-events/subscribe.html

(Current as of February 2020. Of course these landing pages will likely change over time, so reach out if you'd like any updates.)

GET IN TOUCH

In this chapter, we looked at how a strong work ethic is a great thing to have, but still not quite enough when you're chasing government business.

You have to work smarter too. Finding the right balance of stubborn and shrewd takes trial and error (as well as a good hard look in the mirror).

I can't do any of this hard work for you, but I'm happy to give a few pointers. Email me direct at government@ thinqlearning.com.au. I check my inbox every day.

RULE 1

PARTNERS MUST BE ACTIVELY
SOUGHT AND MANAGED – ALWAYS
WITHIN A **WIN:WIN FRAMEWORK**.

CHAPTER TWO

Strength in numbers

SO FAR, YOU'VE READ about how I made the decision to focus on government customers and how I got my head in the game. In this chapter we're going to talk about the different strategies I used to target all three levels of government. Rest assured, I've tried just about every tactic under the sun: phone calls, emails, LinkedIn, meetings. They all played their part. As a matter of fact, they all still do.

One of my dreams, however, saw me being presented with a gloriously big government contract that would reward me with fame and fortune. Well, maybe not the fame. My pursuit of this particular dream involved a four-step routine:

1. Spend a lot of time finding said government contracts.
2. Spend even more time putting together responses that I felt would give my company the edge over our competition.
3. Submit the responses.
4. Alternate between throwing pinches of salt over my left shoulder, closing my eyes when black cats were nearby and stroking rabbits' feet.

Over time, I got better at points one to three, and I came to rely less and less on point four.

THE HUNT

All levels of government really do make it relatively easy for businesses to find those big pieces of work which go to market. Governments usually have a central landing page listing all current and open tenders. Go there and search for work that suits your company. Download as many as you like.

When I first discovered these sites, I was amazed at how much information on government contracts was freely available to anyone. I felt like it would only be a matter of time before I'd be celebrating government success. It all seemed relatively simple.

It wasn't simple. I spent countless hours digging through government documents that, on the outside, looked like winners. Once I really got in and had a good look under the bonnets of the problems that government was trying to solve, it often turned out that my company wasn't really in a position to offer a complete solution. You'll come across this too. For most businesses, less than one percent of all official tender documents released will be in your organisational field of expertise.

You can often wait 12 months or longer for a piece of work to be published that your business has a chance of winning. So, positioning your business to win government tenders as its *primary* revenue driver, without first having established alternative revenue streams which *do not* rely on government, is madness. More on that later.

I didn't know any of this as I pored over the tenders listed on the landing page, but it probably wouldn't have deterred me. If anything, it likely would have motivated me more to prove that I would be the one to crack the code.

So I persevered.

As listed above, step one was finding government work that my company had the resources and capability to fulfil. This was often harder than finding a lonely Smartie in a sea of M&Ms.

Once step one was complete and my excitement died down, a new challenge rolled down the road and hit me hard: my company could often solve only part of the problem. Often, only a small part.

To illustrate I'll completely make up a scenario …

FLYING CARS

Let's say the government realises it has a problem and, for some reason, only a flying car can solve it.

Their next step is to work out what that flying car needs to do in order to solve the problem. A tender document for this flying car solution is then drawn up and sent out to the world.

In this piece of fiction, it just so happens that my company makes really good tyres. The tyres we make are hard-wearing and eco-friendly. They're also more expensive than any other tyre because it's pretty difficult to manufacture an eco-friendly tyre! My company has eight staff and we've been operating solidly for 12 years. We have a small — though loyal and growing — customer base.

One day I stumble across the flying car tender documents. I can clearly see that the contract will be worth a lot to my business. The company they choose will partner with government on this huge project and this will, in turn, help them expand into other government areas. Furthermore, the mainstream attention received would be an asset unto itself.

Unfortunately, the government doesn't want my good green tyres. They want a flying car.

I shake my head sadly, move my mouse over the delete button and click. And just like that I've unknowingly cost my small business the chance to grow at a pace I would never have thought possible.

LOST OPPORTUNITY

How many times in my search for tenders did I find problems to which I could provide only partial solutions? Many.

How many times did I walk away because I knew I didn't have everything in place to fulfil the mandatory requirements? Too many.

How many times did I click delete and cost my company a good shot at solid and profitable government work? I'd prefer not to publish that number.

Now, to a certain extent my actions were correct. In fact, they would be easily defendable in court. This is because unless government believes you can meet all the 'mandatory requirements' that their tender demands, then the likelihood of being selected is virtually zero.

So why bother? And that's exactly what I did. Or didn't do. I didn't bother.

This was yet another alpha mistake of mine, and one that I'd counsel every SMB not to make. It took a while but I eventually learned the error of my ways.

AWAKENING

One day I was on a video call with one of those government contacts I'd made as part of growing my government IQ. We'd known each other for a while by this point and had a good, open rapport. Towards the end of the call, I moaned about a tender doc that I'd gone through the night before: we were simply perfect for it ... well, 20 percent of it.

"Are you still going to put a submission together?" my contact asked with a puzzled look on her face.

"No," I replied. "There are eight mandatory requirements listed, and we can only fulfil two of them."

Her face morphed into the expression you make when someone does or says something incredibly stupid. You know the look.

For the next 10 minutes, she enlightened me about the world of 'collaborative offers', also called 'consortium offers'. I was educated to the fact that government doesn't care if you can't fulfil all of the tender requirements yourself. Turns out, government are more than happy to accept and select single bids that involve several different companies.

What happens is these companies create an alliance by joining together. They know that, separately, they won't be considered for the work, but by coming together like Voltron they can present a much stronger and more compelling proposal that *solves the government's problem*. And that's exactly what government wants: they want the problem solved.

I also learned that when bringing together a consortium bid, it's crucial that *one* company takes the 'lead'. This lead must:

- Oversee the proposal
- Manage all communications with government representatives
- Be available for presentations
- Provide answers to questions related to the proposal.

Government wants to know who to contact when necessary, and they need to know that problems will be addressed and action points will be followed. They *do not* want to manage — or even engage in the same communications with — the two or three or six different companies whose consortium bid has won the piece of government work.

CREATE YOUR OWN VOLTRON

You remember Voltron, of course? The cartoon from the 1980s? The show featured a team of specialists, each of whom piloted a unique robot. When a big baddie came along, the team would link these robots together — each becoming a vital component of a much larger and more effective robot.

Now, history is littered with stories and examples of big beating small — on the sporting field, in the boardroom, on the battlefield. Size, whether in the form of huge player budgets, a multinational distribution operation or a massive army, gives the strength and confidence that few will try to rival. For those foolish enough to try to compete, the chances of victory can seem daunting.

Of course, this isn't always the case. History is also filled with many situations where small slays big. The ancient Greeks versus the Persians, *Australia II* at the 1983 America's Cup, Netflix vs. Blockbuster. How did they do it? Some of it was luck, some of it was capability, some of it was market forces. However, from my experience, one of the key things possessed by the smalls who beat the bigs is better intel.

If my current older, wiser self could travel back in time to advise the bright-eyed, eager-beaver me just starting out, one of the chief pieces of advice I'd give would be: expand your network!

By network, I'm not referring to bumping up one's LinkedIn profile numbers. I'm saying you need to sit down for as long as it takes and make a wish list of companies that don't exactly compete with you, but which might *complement* what your company does.

Make the list as big you want. Once you've got it, sort it and rank it. Start with your "Perfect Partner on Paper" and go right down to "I don't know much about them, but they look like a company to partner with".

Now you have to vet your list. Start at the top and work down the list. Remember, you're looking for potential partners. Look very closely into whether they:

1. Are quality companies
2. Do quality work
3. Are good operators
4. Have solid reputations.

If they tick all four boxes, arrange a meeting with them. If they check out, propose a partnership.

Eventually, you'll forge an alliance of companies that you can confidently partner with when a government contract is released. Over time, you can further refine these partnerships into a cooperative. When complex pieces of government work are released, your cooperative can offer clear and distinct advantages that entice government to pick your small business over another Big Business.

POWERFUL PARTNERS: USE THEM!

I know of a few co-op partnerships that lie dormant, often for a long time, waiting for an innocent and unsuspecting government contract to wander by. The cooperative then pounces, pulling together as much as it can to chase the government business. The tender response unleashes the cooperative's entire combined arsenal. Then they wait for the smoke to clear.

There are only two possible outcomes:

1. They're selected to service the contract and there are high-fives all round
2. They're not selected, the cooperative quietly disbands and the constituent parts go back to watching and waiting for another innocent piece of attractive government work to wander by.

I've often wondered why some companies only harness the power of co-ops when formal government work is announced. Why take the time and effort to form partnerships and create a co-op and yet only use its power randomly? This doesn't make sense.

Increasing the chances of winning a government contract is just one significant advantage of partnering with other organisations. The many other potential benefits include:

- **Growing your contacts database:** You have a database of email subscribers; they have the same. When you send out your next email communication to your list, co-promote a bonus or special for your partner as well. Get them to do the same for you. This can be a quick and simple way to grow your market and inject a revenue boost.
- **Expand value-adds:** Suppose you're a catering company specialising in selling Spanish tapas to the corporate market. Why not partner with a company that specialises in furniture rental and party-hire? Now you can offer their services should any of your clients need tables, chairs, cups and the like. When your clients need these party-hire products and they provide the code you give them they receive a 20 percent discount.
- **Joint venture:** You write a blog that has proven popular and you now have over 5,000 subscribers. Your blog is themed around yoga and all the problems it solves for those who practise regularly. So, you find a company that makes yoga mats and arrange to sell those mats via your blog with a percentage of every mat sale going to you.

No matter what an SMB does, one of its main objectives when starting out should be to create strong and complementary partnerships. Why? Depending on who you talk to, somewhere between 45 and 55 percent of small businesses in Queensland permanently close their doors before seeing their third birthday. I have no doubt that many of those failed businesses didn't feel a partnership strategy was important for the health and future of their company.

Maybe they felt what they offered the market was attractive enough, so why potentially muddy the waters? Maybe they felt partnerships would only bring them headaches and problems. Maybe they didn't even consider partners out of ignorance.

Whatever the reason, it still holds that there is almost always strength in numbers.

If an SMB wants to increase the likelihood that government will notice it and reward it with a profitable contract, it must start forming mutually beneficial partnerships immediately. This is not a nice-to-have thing. Unless you have a niche offering and zero competitors (the possibility of this is pretty low), then good partnerships are a must-have.

If your SMB has made it through start-up to reach profitability and growth without any partners, well done! However, I'd still advise you to find partners right now.

If you're a struggling SMB with no partnerships in place, I'd strongly advise you to build up a partner base immediately. After all, what have you got to lose?

RULE 1

Partners must be actively sought and managed — always within a **win:win framework**.

GET IN TOUCH

In many ways, I hope that finding out about the value of partnerships wasn't the earth-shattering news for you that it was for me.

And, if you want to know more about how you and your business can go about approaching and structuring your partnerships, we'll need to go into specifics. If that's the case, it would be best to just flick me an email: government@ thinqlearning.com.au.

RULE 2

BUILD RELATIONSHIPS WITH AND
LEARN FROM PEERS WHO ALREADY
WORK WITH GOVERNMENT.

CHAPTER THREE

White horses and Jedis

MY FIRST MAJOR BARRIERS to unlocking government revenue streams were simple: I just didn't know how government operated, nor what they looked for in their suppliers and partners. I hoped someone would ride in on a big white horse to nobly take on the time-consuming and complicated challenges of targeting all forms of government business. They'd help me with everything from small pieces of BAU (Business As Usual) work to expressions of interest (EOIs). They'd manage the requests for quotes (RFQs) and grant applications. They'd even deliver government presentations and write large tenders. As you can probably guess, no-one ever did ride in and save me.

Opening government revenue channels takes time. If there's one thing most SMBs lack, it's time. This, combined with the fact that our company lacked the personnel and resources enjoyed by our big national competitors, often drove me to kicking cans. I wondered if I'd ever be able to write regular invoices to a government department.

Eventually I got fed up with the time challenge (as well as not having made any meaningful inroads into government). I decided to find that hero on the big white horse and see what they could do for me. I knew there had to be people who were 'experts' at securing government work, and who, for a price, could do the same for me.

Happily, I was spot on in my thinking — at least I was spot on for one avenue of winning government business.

ARE WHITE HORSES WORTH THE PRICE?

When I went looking for advisors to help me win government work, I soon found several companies claiming to specialise in writing government tenders for the private and not-for-profit sectors. There are many organisations out there that promise to take care of the tender-writing component for you. They say they have the knowledge and the experience. As their websites claim, they'll increase your chances of winning the contract.

When I found them, I was ecstatic. White horses aplenty! This excitement soured once I found out how much these white horses cost. The good ones — and I always look for good suppliers (pay peanuts, get monkeys) — charge anywhere between $10k and $20k for one, yes *one*, decent-sized tender submission. Even after paying this sort of money, the Ts and Cs clearly state there are no guarantees at all of winning and seeing any return.

While the starting price for their services is often less than $15k, once all the variables and extras are factored in the cost can increase very quickly. And that's *per tender response*. For me to justify such a cost I'd need a 100 percent swear-on-your-mother's-life guarantee that we'd be standing on the podium when the winning bid was announced. Alas, that particular guarantee was never forthcoming ...

It seems to me that these white horses are essentially, by design or otherwise, priced in a bracket that only the bigger companies can easily afford. They can be commissioned by big companies to refine and perfect submissions until it's virtually a lock that they'd make the final shortlist. The net result being more government revenue going to Big Business.

I know many SMBs. Very few are in a position to allocate this kind of money for this type of service without an almost iron-clad guarantee of a return.

Where did all this leave me as I looked for a way to unlock government revenue? Still weighing up the time-effort-expense equation.

TIME IS MONEY

The specialist tender and grant-writing companies often advertise that their service usually takes between 10 and 20 days to complete. This not only conveniently justifies the substantial cost, but also allows them to work on several different tenders simultaneously.

Further, the companies that commission these tendering specialists still have to spend a lot of time compiling and providing the documentation and information required for the submission. This list of what might be required for a submission is significant, however it usually includes:

- Company history
- Organisation chart
- Insurances held
- Quality framework held
- Internal processes
- Points of difference
- Price points
- Products
- Awards
- Personnel
- Value-adds.

I looked closely at the service these tendering companies offered. I began to calculate roughly how much of my own time I'd still need to provide even if I was able to hire one of these white horses. I concluded it would still take days out of my BAU. I then worked out what that would cost my business, factoring in the *actual* cost to meet, feed and ride one of the white horses. I decided to let them gallop on by.

What I did instead was respond to tender requests myself. While I wasn't exactly throwing darts blindfolded, it certainly felt like that in the early days. Yet, as one of my brilliant instructors once told me, practice makes progress.

PRACTICE MAKES PROGRESS

"Practice makes perfect" is a proverb worshipped in a world made up of lollipop houses, fairy dust and flying pigs.

No matter how many hours my sons spend practicing their soccer skills in the backyard, they'll never be 'perfect' in the true sense of the word.

No matter how many hours my nephew blows his trombone, he'll never be truly perfect.

No matter how many tenders I submit, I'll never be recognised as 'perfect' at it.

Something else to consider is whether you're doing the 'right practice'. Legendary (and legendarily ethical) journalist Edward R Murrow summed it up best when he said: "We cannot make good news out of bad practice." If your practice is based on flawed theories or techniques, then improving is impossible — you just repeat the same mistakes.

I've since come to believe that "practice makes *progress*" is a more realistic and relevant proverb. Practice makes progress is something I've unashamedly adopted. I frequently say to my three young boys: "Don't give up. Keep practicing. Keep trying. You will improve. Over time you will get better."

Champion golfer Sam Snead once said: "Practice puts brains in your muscles." While I didn't know it at the time, this is exactly what was happening to me in my quest for government revenue streams. I did the right practice. I got better. I refined my submissions and started winning government business — small pieces at first, but from little things ...

No doubt some people will read this and conclude that if I'd bought the white horse then we could have all saved a lot of time, work and lost revenue. I don't agree, however, I have no way to prove it. I chose my path and learned a lot walking down it. On occasions I stumbled. Sometimes I fell over. Frequently it felt like I wasn't making any progress at all.

Yet I got back up and continued on my journey, learning so much along the way. I'd argue this experience helped put my company in a stronger position overall than if they'd just paid an expert.

JEDI MENTOR, ANYONE?

There's a lot of merit to the saying "success is not a destination, it's a journey". On my tender-writing journey, I learned some things that worked and some that didn't. I found out what government looked for in suppliers ... and what types of companies they prefer to avoid. Along the way, I met many great government officials whom I still work with today.

Nonetheless, I often wished I had a Jedi-like mentor who could give short and succinct critiques of my work. The right tip here and there to help me unravel the government puzzle. The right warnings to help me avoid alpha mistakes. Some considered affirmations when I was on the right track. These people are out there. Don't confuse your Jedi and the white horses either: the Jedi is a mentor you have an ongoing relationship with; the white horses are just a means to gallop over the rough spots as you prepare a single grant or tender submission.

If you're an SMB that wants to work with government, begin the search for your Jedi immediately. You may or may not find them. If you do, their guidance will be invaluable. If you don't, the search itself will be most instructive. Don't throw the towel in if you don't find your Jedi; consider them a nice-to-have.

My own journey is far from complete. I'm still learning and growing. I know my road is not for everyone and that's fine. If you can afford a white horse, or maybe a few white horses, then let them take the reins of official government submissions for you. If it's done right, and by the right person, then over time they'll likely deliver you to success. For myself, I realised I didn't have the time or money to buy those horses, so I grew and developed in ways that I feel are more valuable to me. I believe this will also prove important to other SMBs that are looking to secure government works.

Doing it all yourself is the tougher road. It can seem almost impossible to even find where the road begins. In reality, 'where to start' is the simplest question to answer. Once you've committed yourself to seeking government work, you've already taken the first step on the road. Where and how far you go from there is completely up to you. The important thing is to keep taking steps. It's all practice. And practice is progress.

RULE 2

Build relationships with and **learn from peers** who already work with government.

GET IN TOUCH

This chapter makes it clear that, like anything in business, finding government work comes down to a time and money equation.

While it is tempting — and, yes, sometimes necessary — to buy in the expertise, doing the hard yards of practice for yourself sharpens your instincts. Think of the experience as 'IP' where the cost of production are the regular knockbacks.

Yet, if you plan to hunt government work on a regular basis, those instincts will be more useful to you in the long run.

This book encodes my own instincts. If parts of it don't quite gel for you, let me know at government@thinqlearning. com.au.

FOLLOW THE AXIOM THAT
**"MANDATORY DOESN'T ALWAYS
MEAN MANDATORY".**

CHAPTER FOUR

When no means yes

'MANDATORY' HAS MANY CONNOTATIONS in the public and private sector. If you run this word through any common thesaurus, you'll find its synonyms include "compulsory", "required" and "binding". These are all pretty strong words that leave little-to-no grey areas. This is not quite the case in government tendering documentation.

One thing you must do when looking into a formal piece of government work is analyse the "minimum mandatory requirements" section. This is usually the first section I skip to. These requirements list the absolute minimum requirements that must be met for an organisation to be considered for the work. If you meet the minimum mandatory requirements then you're in a good place to ask for the work. If not, then you won't be considered. Makes sense, right?

Wrong.

It took me a long time to figure this out. Until I did, I used the 'minimum mandatory requirements' as my pulse-check to determine whether to bid or not. It was another alpha mistake.

IT'S NOT ALL MANDATORY.
WELL IT IS, BUT IT ISN'T ...

Looking back, I can readily admit that our company passed on many pieces of government work that we likely could have won. Often, we'd be mostly capable of delivering the product or service, but just lacked a few of these 'mandatory' conditions. So we shrugged our shoulders resignedly and moved on.

Several tenders we disregarded because we didn't have any ISO 14001 Environmental Management System in place. Many contracts we ignored as we didn't have a branch office in a regional area. More government contracts we skipped as we were missing one particular certification on scope. We could get the certification on scope, but it would take eight weeks to do so and the deadline for submissions didn't allow that luxury.

Here's a current example: at the time of writing, the Department of Housing and Public Works are looking for a company to deliver cleaning services to some government buildings in Emerald. Most of what they need is pretty standard office cleaning, however as part of the service, the company selected must: "Thoroughly machine scrub loading bays, delivery/waste collection areas and main entries. Resulting sludge removed with a wet and dry vacuum." So, essentially a company will not meet the minimum requirement unless they have a machine that will scrub and clean the loading docks.

There will be many pieces of government work that you will come across and discard because the 'must have' requirements seem too onerous for your small business, or too costly to invest in without a guarantee of a return. When this happens, I want you to stop and do a little exercise: grab a pen and paper and come up with some creative ways that you could deliver the work.

1. What would you need to buy or hire to complete the brief? Would you need to employ any new people? Make note of the extra resources you'd need in order to put forward your submission. Calculate how much these extra resources would cost your business.
2. Determine how much that piece of government work will be worth and how much profit you will make. I'd recommend using a worst-case scenario method.
3. Think of the impact these extra purchases could have on your business. Will they help you win other work that you have previously ignored? Will you see more revenue from existing customers by adding a new product or service line?
4. Sit back and see the whole scenario for what it really is.

Now you're in a position to make a clear decision to either fight for the government work or let it go and move on. You might not meet the stipulations today, but so long as you could show you would be able to meet them should you win the tender, you can still proceed with your submission.

Back to our example: Just because a cleaning company might not have a machine that can scrub and clean loading bays doesn't mean it can't bid for — and win — a tender that requires such. What they would need to do is provide supporting evidence that they will have the right machine by the required date. They'd then meet the mandatory requirement. The best way to go about providing this evidence is relatively simple.

First, formalise an agreement with the company that sells these machines. In the agreement terms be sure to outline that you will purchase this machine within the required timeframe and that it will also be delivered within this timeframe. When you include this agreement in your response, you effectively fulfil the mandatory requirement. If you win the government business, you go ahead and place the order. If you don't, then you have the option of not proceeding with the machine purchase.

When I finally understood this, it was a revelation. Cue massive lightbulb turning on. Sirens blaring. Clouds parting. Pick whatever metaphor you like. Suddenly, a much bigger world of government work opened up to me. I could foresee so much more government business we could tender submissions for.

Be warned: you have to follow through. It is not a good look to be awarded a contract and then refuse to service it because you can't find the machine or can't afford it. You do not want a reputation within government circles as being *that* company.

BIG BUSINESS KNOWS

Since my revelation, I've asked a lot of SMBs if they knew that mandatory wasn't *technically* mandatory. It was about a 50/50 split between those who knew and those who didn't.

Out of curiosity, I also discussed this with a few contacts who are well-established and high-ranking within large national and multinational companies. Did these professionals involved in tender responses know that mandatory wasn't quite mandatory? Absolutely. Several of them even volunteered real situations when they had used the fact to help win large pieces of work. I don't know how many SMBs have passed on bidding for government work due to not meeting all 'mandatory' requirements. Considering there are over 400,000 SMBs in Queensland alone, I'd say it would be a lot.

Some of you reading this might now decide to go back through past tenders that you have let slide because you didn't have all of the mandatory requirements. You'll find many lucrative government contracts that you could have bid for but decided against. Unless you enjoy regret, don't do this. There's little point. Those ships have been given to your competition who sailed away with them long ago. Instead, keep your eyes out for new fleets on the horizon — some will arrive quickly, others will take a while.

Find the ships that suit you. Find the ships you can sail. And never, ever, forget that mandatory doesn't always mean mandatory.

RULE 3

Follow the axiom that **"mandatory doesn't always mean mandatory"**.

GET IN TOUCH

Now you know that going for government business is not always what you have to offer, but what you can guarantee to have to offer, as long as you have supporting evidence.

Governments understand that the opportunities they present rarely suit any business perfectly. So, if making your submission today means you'll have to make that solution happen tomorrow, then so be it. It's just imperative that you provide clear evidence and follow it through.

And, if you're stumped on how to pull that off, get in touch — I might have a few ideas for you: government@ thinqlearning.com.au.

PRIORITISE CRITERIA ACCORDING
TO THEIR **WEIGHTING**.

CHAPTER FIVE

Do the math

I'VE ALWAYS WANTED TO BE a woodworker. I'm that guy who almost subconsciously gravitates to the "wood-man stand" at the local markets. I marvel at how these Wood Gods can transform a chunk of nondescript old timber into a beautiful and useful piece that people pay good money for. For most of my life I've struggled to even paint a piece of wood, let alone work it.

Regardless, a Wood God is what I want to be. Well maybe not a Wood God exactly, I just want to be good enough to claim woodworking as a retirement hobby. I imagine myself trundling up to the local market every Sunday morning to show off my wares. If I sell some, happy days. If not, there's more pepper grinders and salad bowls under the Christmas tree.

Before I could do this, I would first need the skills to create something from nothing. I'd need training. Yet, whenever I'd get to the stage of choosing a wood-working school that could teach me those skills, I'd back out and cite lack of time as the main reason. In hindsight, it wasn't a lack of time at all: it was more fear of the unknown. Fear of failure. Fear of embarrassing myself. But that's a whole other book and not relevant right now.

Anyway, one day, out of nowhere, I surprised myself. I actually pulled the trigger and picked the company who'd teach me about all things wood. I enrolled in a course that had me building a coffee table from scratch over seven consecutive Sunday afternoons. This was a pretty big step for me. I couldn't nail straight let alone use drop saws, Japanese saws, planers and routers. Yet here I was hoping to produce a coffee table masterpiece that actually functioned. Secretly, I felt there was the distinct possibility that I was spending $400 building something that would end up being very expensive firewood on our next family camping trip.

Yet I'm proud that I finished the course. I loved every minute of it. I remember one particular session where I learnt a lot from making a mistake.

At the time, I was using a hand plane to work the wood at the top inside of the table legs. When I'm woodworking, my concentration levels are really high because it's all so new for me. I often lose track of time. So I was startled when my wood-working-ninja-legend-mentor Rob, tapped me on the shoulder.

"Tom, what's taking so long?" Rob asked in his blunt, old-school way.

I looked around and saw that everyone else was on the next step of finishing the tabletop to be ready for the big final assembly. I showed Rob what I was doing. He told me to stop right now and move onto the tabletop.

"There's no need to spend so long making the leg top look perfect, because, once we assemble, no-one will ever see it," Rob said. "Just make it flat and square. It's more important to spend time on making the tabletop look the best it can. That's where all the action is when you're a coffee table."

FOCUS ON THE NECESSARY

My woodworking mistake — spending too much time on the unnecessary — is similar to one many small businesses make when they submit for government work.

When government goes to market looking for the solution to a problem, they often include what they call a "selection criteria" or "evaluation criteria". Often these criteria are spelt out and weighted by percentages. Sometimes, it's not weighted specifically, but by reading the request for quote (RFQ), expression of interest (EOI), tender outlines and so on you can get a pretty good idea of what's more important. Here's a basic example:

Sample evaluation criteria

EVALUATION CRITERIA AND COMMENTS	WEIGHTING
Supplier experience and capability The supplier will be evaluated on their overall experience and capability in delivering similar past projects.	30%
Project management The supplier will be evaluated on their processes related to project management and service delivery.	10%
Local benefits The supplier will be evaluated on: • the number of local jobs supported by the procurement activity • use of local contractors, manufacturers and supply chain directly relating to the supply of goods and/or services • the number of local apprentices and trainees supported by the procurement activity • the number of local Aboriginal jobs and Torres Strait Islander jobs supported by the procurement activity.	20%
Price The supplier will be evaluated on their offered price.	40%

A lot of SMBs trip up here. They don't spend enough time on the sections that are weighted most heavily. Instead, they allocate too much time and effort to areas that are minimally weighted — or worse, not weighted at all. I've seen it happen first hand.

A colleague once asked me to read over and offer any suggestions to a tender response she had completed and was about to submit. The tender was for around $350k in estimated services over 12 months. So a decent chunk of reliable revenue spread out over a year. I took it away and spent a few hours going over the tender document and the information she'd included. It was really flashy: lots of diagrams, pretty colours, beautiful design and a *lot* of content.

However, when I drilled down and compared her submission against the tender's evaluation criteria, I realised quickly that we had no chance of winning the tender. None at all.

I went back to the BDM and gave her my honest thoughts. I am a huge fan of honesty, but occasionally I have been known to deliver some communications a bit too ... let's say, brutally. She curtly thanked me for my opinion, and I went back to my work. A few weeks later I was told that our company had received the "Dear John/Jane" email informing us that we'd been knocked out in the first round of culling, but thanks so much for your interest ...

While our submission looked fantastic on the surface, we hadn't actually aligned or weighted our *response* to the *evaluation criteria*. The evaluation criteria which had been spelt out in black and white — even in a larger font, from memory. Essentially, our company had spent a lot of time planing the top of the coffee-table leg and nowhere near enough time on the tabletop.

We'd provided masses of detail around three or four areas that were weighted at under 10 percent. Further, there was plenty of information on things that weren't part of the evaluation criteria at all. To compound the problem, we were also very light in two areas that were weighted at 20 percent and 30 percent respectively — pretty major criteria.

When this sort of thing happens, it sends one of two clear messages to government:

1. We aren't really capable of performing the work: we're covering it up by going large on the secondary points.
2. Our organisation is incompetent: we didn't even read the brief properly.

It's so vital to align all tender submissions directly with the evaluation criteria. Ignore this at your peril. If, in the past, you've not been successful in even getting considered for government work, there's a good chance you have fallen into this trap.

If a tender selection criteria lists one criteria weighted at 50 percent, then the rough rule is that around half of your tender response should be devoted to that criteria. A 50 percent weighting means that criteria is extremely important to government. They're asking you to give it a lot of love and attention. You need to make your response sing!

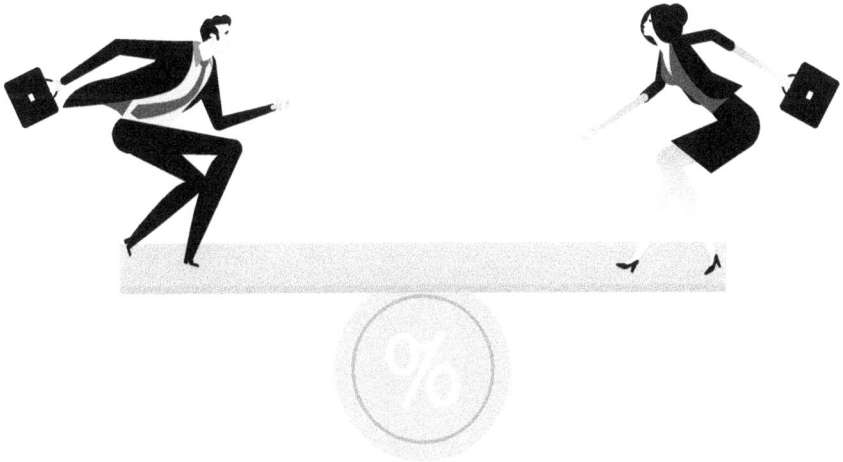

YOU ONLY THRIVE IF YOU FIRST SURVIVE

When it comes to awarding contracts, the companies that are left standing in the final round are usually the ones who have scored highly in areas that are weighted heavily. So, when assessing your suitability for a piece of government work, the question is: can you put a strong and creative case forward in the heavyweight areas?

If yes, then you must consider making a submission for the work. If no, don't immediately write it off. Look to your partnerships to cover any shortfalls. Perhaps read chapter two again.

When you start approaching the criteria weightings in this manner, you're making it easier for the selection committee to look favourably on you. Why? While you can be sure they'll look at every part of your submission, they'll only give the 'legs' a quick check to see if they're flat and square. They do this so they have more time to really pay attention to the 'tabletop' — that is, the criteria where the action is.

RULE 4

Prioritise criteria according to their **weighting**.

GET IN TOUCH

Picking your battles is about more than just choosing a path to commit yourself to, it's about choosing where to place your foot at every step on that path too.

That's the core message I am trying to get across here: the weightings specifically identify which ones the good battles are.

If you're currently looking at a set of criteria weightings and can't quite decipher what's what, feel free to shoot me a quick email: government@thinqlearning.com.au.

RULE 5

STAY THE COURSE. YOU WILL
NOT SUCCEED WITH YOUR FIRST
ATTEMPT.

CHAPTER SIX

Persist or perish

MOST COMPANIES THAT DISCOVER the secret sauce and unlock government revenue streams have usually failed in *many* previous attempts. How does that saying go? "Nothing worth having comes easy." Or we can look to Winston Churchill who once summed it up perfectly: "Success is stumbling from failure to failure with no loss of enthusiasm."

So many companies give up on the hunt for their 'biggest unicorn' after only a handful of setbacks or rejections. They put so much work into one or two submissions. They spend enormous amounts of time — which, as we've noted, they're usually already short of — fine-tuning and refining their 100-page proposal. They produce a small novel that's so perfect that surely government must choose them this time. And yet, weeks later, they receive the crushing news that they've been culled out in Round One, but "thanks so much for sending through your proposal and please submit again next time".

After receiving a handful of those "Dear John/Jane" letters from different government departments, the disgruntled and disillusioned SMB packs it in and puts potentially lucrative and regular government streams in the too-hard basket. They talk themselves into believing that government won't ever see the value and benefits of working with them. They tell themselves that government is too much of a dinosaur to understand the cost and time savings that their superior product or service provides. They conclude that government business is just not for them.

This is a trap that so many SMBs fall into. This is also a trap that Big Business welcomes because it removes their smaller and more nimble competitors from bidding and allows them to inflate their prices. Big Business loves it when another SMB throws in the towel: it means almost certain growth for them.

However, there is a lot to be said for grit and persistence. I'll tell you a story to illustrate what I mean. Years ago I placed a job ad. I needed to expand the sales team so the company began searching for the right person with the right culture and the right experience.

HE NEVER GAVE UP

I remember one resume and cover letter in particular. No, this person wasn't the one for me: he'd jumped around from job to job the last five years — never staying more than 10 months in the same position. He had limited sales experience and none in account management. He'd spent no real time in the sector that our company lived and breathed. He did, however, have a very good cover-letter. It was articulate, persuasive, and made it clear that he really wanted the opportunity to work with our team and prove his worth.

I sent him back a polite response thanking him for his interest and letting him know that he'd not made the cut for the second interview stage. Over the next nine months the same resume with a slightly tweaked cover letter arrived in my inbox on no less than six separate occasions. The first five times I replied with a similar response to my original. However, on his sixth attempt I stopped and thought about him from a different perspective. I thought about how determined he was. I thought about the hard edge required to take the constant rejection and yet continue knocking on the door. I thought about the *character* of someone who could do that day-in and day-out.

I realised these were all qualities that I admired. They were qualities I looked for in my people. They were also qualities necessary to be successful in the BDM role. I phoned him and told him that while I didn't think he was completely suited for the role, I admired his persistence and that, if he'd like to come in for an interview, then I was happy to book a time.

Two days later we met.

One day later I offered him the role.

Three years later and after many successes, my team gave him a big farewell party after a multinational made him an offer too good to refuse.

From day one this guy had worked his butt off to learn the role. He listened. He attached himself to his team leader and absorbed everything he could. He role-played. He practiced. He tried. He failed. He tried again. Most importantly, he applied what he learned in 'the real world'. Very quickly, as his can-do character asserted itself, he became a key member of the team. His activity levels remained high. Soon enough, he began making his monthly and quarterly targets. He continued his learning and applying journey. Soon enough, he was smashing his targets.

TOUGHING IT OUT

I often tell the above story to people who I believe might benefit from its lessons. First, they learn about the difficult journey of someone who went from nothing to become one of our best BDMs. Second, and more important, it highlights the danger that assumptions can lead to terrible decisions. If that young man hadn't kept knocking on my door, I never would've opened it. I'd like to think that I haven't made that mistake again ... but I'm only human.

Obviously, I'm not the only one to have made a mistake like this. Some had much bigger ramifications. In 1995, JK Rowling completed the first of her *Harry Potter* novels. Then, needing a publisher, she set about the task of finding the right one to promote and distribute her work. She was rejected by 12 — yes 12 — publishers. Only lucky 13, a then-small printing house called Bloomsbury purchased the manuscript. Rowling is now a billionaire.

Another example: at the time of writing, there are some 23,000 KFC restaurants and outlets in 119 countries. However, in the beginning, Colonel Sanders — already in his 60s — drove thousands of kilometres around the United States looking for someone to purchase his chicken recipe. He went from one restaurant to the next cooking batches of his chicken for restaurant owners and employees to taste. The Colonel suffered through 1009 rejections before he got a yes. Read that again: 1009 rejections before the drought broke.

Here's another: Dr Donald Unger wanted to prove to his mother-in-law and to his aunt that regularly cracking your knuckles didn't lead to arthritis. Using himself as the control specimen, he cracked the knuckles on his left hand twice every day ... for 50 years. After 36,500 cracks, his left hand was still arthritis free. His persistence paid off when, in 2009, he won an Ig Nobel Prize — an annual award for unorthodox scientific experiments. And, happiest of all, he'd proved his mother-in-law wrong.

While there are many reasons SMBs are unsuccessful in winning government work, a lack of persistence is one of the most common. It's an essential ingredient that all SMBs must have if they want to crack the government nut.

If you can't grit your teeth and climb back up off the canvas, bloodied and bruised after yet another rejection from government, then I'd advise you to not even climb into the ring. Opening new, regular and potentially highly profitable government revenue streams — to ride the biggest unicorn — requires serious effort and a whole lot of persistence. However, once you have your foot in the door and government begins to trust you, it is far easier to win more government work. You just need to stay the course.

RULE 5

Stay the course. You will not succeed with your first attempt.

GET IN TOUCH

There's a chance you've got more grit in chasing government work than your boss has patience for results. In fact, because it can take so long, this is highly likely!

If the choice to hang in there is out of your hands, get in touch. I'll give a bit of advice about how to explain to your boss that winning government work is often a gradual thing and that when it pays off, it can pay off handsomely. Email me at: government@thinqlearning.com.au.

RULE 6

IT ALL STARTS WITH A **PHONE CALL**.

It all starts with a phone call

THE FOLLOWING SECTION IS all about reaching for the low-hanging fruit. So, let's talk about Business As Usual (BAU) revenue. I refer to BAU as "government business acquired through standard day-to-day, or month to month, operations". Say a government department is hosting a lunch meeting with industry experts and they need catering. They engage a caterer. Say a few people in the finance team need to update their Excel skills. The team manager reaches out to an IT trainer.

BAU work is usually smaller in size than tenders or grants. It also often doesn't require the SMB to be on any preferred government supplier panel or Standing Offer Arrangement (SOA). If a product or service costs less than $10k, most government departments can engage a supplier without having to go through the often-rigorous and time-consuming formal selection process.

Imagine BAU as the low-hanging fruit of government business. It's certainly not as big as the jackfruit higher up the tree, but it's far more plentiful. And importantly for SMBs, it's much easier to reach and consume. What's more, delivering BAU work is easier to uncover and there is less red tape inhibiting an SMB's ability to engage.

So, while BAU is smaller in size, if you are successful at picking up several pieces of BAU, over time it could result in higher revenues and profit than larger and more complex pieces of government business. This begs the immediate question of how you ferret it out. The answer is in your pocket.

YOUR PHONE: USE IT!

Almost all of the BAU revenue I have secured in the government sector began with a humble phone call. I am not referring to a 'hard sell' call, or even a 'soft call' sell. I'm talking about a simple and basic 'intro call'. I emphasise, this call is *basic*. So basic that many people I advise to make such calls don't believe they'll achieve anything. Your intro call isn't designed to garner any commitment from the government contact taking the call. It's not designed to immediately increase sales pipelines. It's not designed to uncover any short-term opportunity or potential business.

This intro call is designed to do exactly what it says: simply and succinctly *introduce* your company and what it does. The secondary function is to ensure that you're talking to the right person or area. This matters because, if required in future, that person will make (or influence) the decision to use your company's product or services over someone else's. The intro call is where you plant the relationship seed that could one day bear BAU fruit, or something even bigger.

The intro call is soft in nature — too soft for most to consider it of any value. However, in these times, where government officials are being inundated from every angle and communications medium, this soft intro call is the most crucial action that SMBs can make towards uncovering government BAU work.

Broken down, the intro call has nine basic steps:

1. Locate the decision maker

The act of locating the decision maker (DM) is undertaken and executed at your point of *entry* into the account. You have to find who within the target department can press the green light to engage your SMB. Once you know who they are, you need to talk to them. Now, a lot of people dismiss the 'receptionist', believing them to have no real power. Big mistake. Without doubt, the receptionist is one of the most important contacts for your SMB. After all, they're the ones who decide if you get through to the DM you need to speak to. Treat receptionists with love and respect and they will help you reach other key people of interest, as well as provide key departmental intel. Let's assume the receptionist puts you through to the DM you're seeking.

2. Confirm the DM

Once past the gatekeeper and in touch with your target DM, it's important to offer a brief introduction of who you are and the company you're representing. This step is to confirm with the DM that they are in fact the *actual* DM. This is essential as it ensures you're speaking with the person who could, if required, decide to engage with you. As a basic example, say I'm trying to confirm if someone is the DM to authorise the purchase of new stationery. What you'd say is as basic and direct as this: "If your department needed new stationery, would you be the person who could make a final decision on that?" Sometimes you might not get complete confirmation. Sometimes you'll have been put through to the person who actually coordinates the new purchase, and not the authoriser. If so, just run with it and continue to the next stage of the call.

3. Current process to buy

Once their DM status is confirmed, you need to ask the person basic questions around how they currently make purchases. Do they source internally; do they have a preferred supplier; do they look for suppliers when required? You might need to prompt them here and offer a couple of examples. Listen intently to their responses. You're trying to get some overall idea of how they buy. Be warned, you won't always get a 100 percent accurate answer. At this point, the DM will still be waiting for your hard sell. This, however, won't happen.

4. Listen loudly

This might sound obvious, and it is. However, most people miss this critical step on an intro call — they fail to offer a well thought out listening statement once the DM has answered the sales process question. A listening statement is where you acknowledge what they've just said — perhaps you sum up their overall concerns or speak their central point back to them — "So, what I'm hearing here is ... [insert statement]. Is this correct?". Listening statements are crucial because they reinforce to the DM that you're a real person and not some robotic cold-caller in an off-shore call centre. By offering a listening statement you also confirm to potential prospects that you're genuinely interested in what they have to say. In short, that you're not only listening to them but you're also *hearing* them.

5. Summarise your company and offerings — succinctly

Now, offer two to three sentences *max* on what your business does and any distinct differentiators. The key here is to summarise your key benefits, not your offering's features. This must be short and to the point — and not salesy.

6. Seek permission to email info

Politely request the DM's permission to email them through your contact details as well as a company info flyer. Ask them to reach out if they have a need in future.

7. Request a touch point

Very casually ask the contact if they'd mind you reaching out from time to time to let them know if anything new comes up that you think could be of interest to them. If delivered correctly, this line will give you the all-clear to contact them in the future. This is key. It will allow you to build a relationship with them over time, so that when they're in the Two Percent Zone (which we'll explain soon), you're the first person they think of contacting. Be careful not to contact them too often. I recommend one touch point every 60 days.

8. Wrap it up

Be conscious of the DM's time. The entire intro call should take no longer than two to three minutes, so once you've achieved point seven it's time to wrap it up. Politely thank the DM for their time. Reaffirm any action points that you have mentioned. For example, clarify that they will receive an email from you shortly.

9. Follow through

Within 15 minutes of ending the call, send them a personalised email with your contact details along with a company flyer or promotional material.

Follow this guide and your intro call will be the polar opposite of the sales calls the DM normally receives. You're simply introducing yourself and your business and asking permission to send them your details should they have need sometime in the future.

Your intro call nails the brief when the DM leaves the call with the sense that you aren't some hard seller looking for quick wins. If the intro call has been delivered well, the DM will be open to talking with you more when you reach out from time to time. And they'll definitely remember you when they're in the Two Percent Zone.

THE TWO PERCENT RULE

The chances of a government Decision Maker needing the exact product or service you offer at the precise moment you make the intro call to them is minuscule. Say you sell red staplers that look like apples, and the precise moment you manage to speak to a government DM on an intro call, they need a red stapler shaped like an apple — how likely is that? You must be aware of this truth and respect it, as it sets the tone and agenda for every intro call.

This reality should remove the temptation to go for the hard sell. It's simply not necessary and will only put you and your business in the same place as so many other companies hawking their wares to government. This is where so many SMBs go wrong with government accounts. If they have no need of your product now, then pushing your wares on them will be about as welcome as Emperor Palpatine turning up to the Rebels' Christmas party.

It's far better to assume the Two Percent Rule, which my old boss once explained to me: only around two percent of the time will a DM need your offering. This being the case, the intro call must assume the DM does *not* need your service when you first speak with them. So, the real goal is to get the DM's permission for you to contact them in future. Once you have this, you have an opportunity to build a trusting relationship with the DM.

When three days, three months or three years later, that DM arrives in the Two Percent Zone, that relationship securely positions you as the first person they contact. Further, even if your prices are higher than your competitors, DMs who trust and know you will find ways to do business with you.

WHERE TO FROM HERE?

Once the intro call has been completed, you'll need to reach out to these government DMs with meaningful insights every 60 to 90 days. The key word here is *meaningful* — that is, meaningful to their needs, not yours. These communications can come in many forms, including:

- Invitations to webinars
- Reports
- Topical stories of interest
- LinkedIn links
- Updated pricing
- New product or service releases from your business
- Industry insights
- Profile call.

Once the DMs understand that your communications aren't pushing a sale, then you're in the right place. After four or five touch points, perhaps request a meeting. A face-to-face meeting will further reinforce trust in you. Remember: people usually like to do business with people they like. A meeting will help reinforce the professional relationship and aims to ensure that when they need your product or service, you will be top of mind.

INTRO CALL OR INTRO EMAIL?

Since the advent of email communications and professional social platforms like LinkedIn, I've had many SMBs tell me that intro phone calls have followed the lead of fax machines, rotary phones, and Blockbuster video stores. Rather, they say digital technologies and online strategies are far more effective in reaching and engaging Decision Makers.

I couldn't disagree more.

I'll go so far as to say I can't see a time when this will ever be the norm. Regardless of all the communication tools available, we are still all human beings who, deep down, desire meaningful human contact. The keyword here again is *meaningful*. I believe that most people still prefer to do business with real people. Preferably people they like.

I receive at least two emails every day from people I've never heard of trying to get me to buy their product or service. They purchased my email address, name and probably my job title from some lead-list company that claims I'm part of a certain 'target market'. These emails usually go something like this:

Good morning Thomas,

Have you recently reviewed your agreements on your company's photocopying equipment? We've found companies in Brisbane are paying too much for unreliable equipment.

As an example, if you're not paying, as an organisation, 5 cents for a colour print, it may be time to review.

Understanding you may be involved in a current agreement with your current supplier, fortunately we have resources in place to finalise these agreements so you can move on with the savings and more efficient devices.

Photocopiers is not all we do, as an example we can streamline accounts payable, docusign (Digital signature), E-forms, IT Services — just to name a few. We provide business solutions essential for our customers to focus on their core business. This is achieved through a broad portfolio of document technology, services, software and supplies.

Can I help you review your current equipment agreements and see if there is room for improvement?

Does Wednesday or Thursday next week suit?

Look forward to your response,

Business Development Manager

You know what my response is? I click delete after reading the first line — often I don't even read that far. They don't have a clue who I am or what my needs are. They don't have a clue if I can sign off on a new photocopier ... or anything else for that matter.

They also have no idea that 18 months ago a rep called Julie from a little local print shop reached out and introduced herself to me. She followed up by sending me a brochure. Since then Julie has called with a few updates on new innovations in print technology, including 3D. Julie's also invited me to a webinar that outlined how 25 percent of printing costs could be eliminated by employing a 'print-on-demand' process.

A couple of months back we met for coffee. She asked me some good questions and I gave her an understanding of how we used our printers and the load on them. I like how Julie operates, and she has always been honest with what her company can and cannot do. In six months I will be in the two percent zone. I'll pick up the phone and call her. Julie will likely have a very quick and simple sale.

There is no point contacting potential DMs to just shout your product from the rooftops and explain directly why they should do business with you. This will only yield zero return on your time investment. Instead, SMBs that take the time to reach out to government officials, politely introduce themselves and seek permission for future contact will almost always set the wheels in motion for future business, big or small.

Always start with a phone call and follow it up with meaningful touch points. These can be a mix of phone calls, emails and face-to-face meetings. Forget what you have heard or believe about targeting government DMs and business via mass emails to government lists. Just pick up the phone and make the call.

I don't care how many times you do this each day.

I don't care if you feel like doing it or not.

I don't care if you get someone else to pick up the phone and begin the intro calls.

I only care that you do it.

Never forget this axiom:

Everything starts with a phone call. Everything.

STAY THE COURSE

If you make intro calls part of your daily or weekly routine, prepare yourself.

There will be many times when you throw your hands up, screaming internally with frustration, because you're not seeing any immediate return.

There will be many times you question the effectiveness and value of picking up the phone and making these calls.

There will be many times when you'll be tempted to return to the mass-marketing lists that are constantly being waved in front of desperate and struggling SMBs.

Yet, I promise that staying the course and maintaining the process will, over time, be infinitely more effective and lucrative than all the government snake-oil methods thrust in front of you combined. For those with the fortitude to consistently make these intro calls and follow-up with touchpoints, you *will* see positive results from your work. You must trust that your work will pay off as government BAU work begins coming your way.

You will receive incoming calls from your growing government network with requests for business.

You will receive payments from government departments that you have taken the time to develop relationships with.

You will open government revenue streams.

The beautiful thing about BAU is that once it's opened, it's hard to turn it off. If you're able to fulfil requests and deliver a quality product and service, then government will continue to buy from you. They will also recommend you onto other departments — and more BAU will follow.

PEOPLE LIKE PEOPLE

Accept the fact that human beings still like to talk to and do business with human beings. Set yourself apart from big and small businesses alike by being a person who treats government contacts like real people. Engage with them like businesses used to: first with a phone call and a simple conversation.

It might feel like you are stepping back in business time. In fact, it's the opposite: companies are forever looking for the easiest and quickest path to source new revenue streams. This has resulted in what I call "The Age of Cyber Selling" — the business equivalent of throwing darts blind-folded. Smart SMBs realise this and have already begun personalising and reinforcing their professional relationships. Smart SMBs know that building trust is the foundation of future business, and this has never been truer in the government sector.

Smart SMBs understand this: people still like to do business with people.

RULE 6

It all starts with a **phone call**.

GET IN TOUCH

Chapter 7 is all about making things easy for your government contacts. It's about positioning yourself, being human and accepting the little jobs. And, when you re-engage, you have to make it worth their while.

It might pay to have a long hard think about what sort of material will make for a meaningful time expenditure to the people you're trying to talk to.

I've been on the other end of this sort of outreach many times, so get in touch with any ideas you want to run by me: government@thinqlearning.com.au.

ABSOLUTE 1

GOVERNMENTS PREFER SMBs WITH
REAL-WORLD CRED. YOU NEED A
PRIVATE-SECTOR TRACK RECORD.

CHAPTER EIGHT

Never start with the unicorn

IF YOU TAKE ONE THING away from this chapter, make it this: companies with products and services that have been created to sell specifically to government are almost always destined to fail. Do not open a business that solely targets government. Why? It all comes down to one simple, yet very powerful word. Risk. Or *perceived* risk might be a better term.

RISKY BUSINESS

History is filled with examples of people taking enormous gambles that have paid off. Jeff Bezos took a huge risk when he chucked in his high-paying job on Wall Street and opened a little online store in his garage. Today Bezos runs the largest company the world has ever seen.

Henry Ford pioneered risk when he reduced working hours for his staff and increased their minimum wage. Conventional wisdom at the time said this would send him broke. Instead he made the equivalent of US$200 billion in today's dollars.

Richard Branson is often thought of as one of the biggest risk-takers of his era. Back in the 1970s, Branson was deep in debt and constantly being chased by banks demanding repayment, yet he continued signing artists and establishing Virgin Records. Today, Branson is a billionaire and the overall Virgin Group has become a global conglomerate employing thousands of people.

Many ambitious risk-takers have gone on to be mega-successful pioneers of their industry. However, it's also a fact that far more companies don't get it right and close their doors. Blockbuster Video and Lehman Brothers are just two examples of big players that most thought would continue to thrive — instead they very publicly failed.

When you look at SMB survival rates, loud alarm bells start sounding. According to the Small Business Association, almost 50 percent of new businesses fail in their first five years. So, how do you avoid this common fate?

EARN YOUR STRIPES

So what do the risk-takers like Branson, Bezos and Ford have in common? The complete answer would fill another book on its own. However, for the purposes of this point, the one common rule they all followed in their formative years was not being reliant on any government business or contracts in order to survive.

They plied their trade in the private sector.

They put their necks on the line in the private sector.

They worked hard in the private sector.

They grew their companies in the private sector.

Why did these leading entrepreneurs spend little to no time targeting government in their formative years? Simply, governments don't enjoy taking unnecessary risks.

To illustrate: Imagine two companies presenting their solutions to government, each with similar pricing. One has a long trading history and many references and case studies. The other is new to the market and only been operating for 12 months with an inexperienced management team. Having to pick one, nine times out of 10 the decision will go to the experienced company because they have a strong track record. They have the experience. They have evidence of successful implementations. They have proven themselves. And so, they get the contract.

A PERSONAL CASE STUDY

One day many years ago, my then girlfriend (who later, amazingly, agreed to marry me) told me she wanted to buy and run a coffee shop in the inner-west of Sydney. She painted a wonderful picture of a bustling shop full of satisfied and regular clientele sipping happily at their freshly-prepared cups of wonderful coffee. What's more, this shop wouldn't just sell great coffee; it would have an irresistible selection of cakes, slices and other treats best served with a quality cuppa.

Not long prior to this conversation I'd read some horror statistics concerning cafés going bust. From memory, it was something horrendous like 60 to 70 percent folding within the first two years of opening. Life savings gone. Marriages wrecked. Misery aplenty. At that time, it was also a fact that we had no real experience in owning any business, let alone a coffee shop. Granted, my girlfriend had consumed many coffees in shops. Still, there was no real brand or experience to rely on. What's more, there were limited cash reserves to fall back on after the initial purchase. I saw the entire dream as a tremendous risk. Sure, there was a chance that if the stars aligned and everything fell into place, that this shop could be the next Starbucks.

However, my head and my heart told me the chances of that happening were vanishingly slim. There was too much stacked against it. Rightly or wrongly, I steered her away from the coffee-shop-running game. I foresaw the very likely result that all the money she had saved would be quickly burned in a venture that, while it might not have been *destined* to fail, faced very short odds of going under. It was just too risky.

PERCEPTION IS REALITY

When you're dealing with government, perception matters. Governments don't want to be — or rather don't want to be *perceived as* — risk-takers. After all, any risks they take are likely to be on the public purse. It's our tax-paying dollars that governments are using and budgeting. And no, not all risk pays off. Much of it doesn't — that's the risk itself. A government that gets a reputation for taking risks that don't pay off will likely be marched over to the Opposition benches come election time when the people decide.

Even if they take some risks that do result in happy outcomes, governments are left with the age-old customer service fact: a bad experience is shared with 10 to 15 people, while a good experience is shared with maybe one or two. Why? Because good experiences are expected, and bad experiences are not. Further, Lindsay Bridger of business skills training firm Bridging Performance notes that heightened emotion makes experiences memorable, which is why people remember bad customer experiences in vivid detail.

Some argue that the old saying of "bad news travels much faster and wider than good" no longer applies since the advent of social platforms. I disagree. Bad experiences will always be shared more often because they aren't expected. Further, with the advent of so-called 'social influencers', people are beginning to doubt positive reviews — it's too easy to believe someone's been paid off to hype a product.

This relates to our discussion of government taking on risk. When government takes on risks that don't pay off, you know everyone will hear about it. Not just by the Opposition, but mainly by traditional and social media platforms which spread the news far quicker than word-of-mouth was ever able to. The effects can be devastating. Sadly, the risks taken that produce positive outcomes are often lost in the noise.

Smart businesses know that government will almost always lean towards suppliers who put their own hand up and take on perceived and apparent risks. This is a key point. If you can provide evidence reinforcing that you're one of them, government will love you for it. If you, as an SMB, absorb relevant risks for a piece of government work, and your competition doesn't, then you have a significant leg up.

Smart businesses also know that in order to work with government, they first need to show that their business can survive in 'the real world' — aka the private sector. Real world experience tests your business model, your management and your offering. It shows you where your deficiencies are and forces you to make improvements. You must get your marketing right, your product right and your service right. All while building the foundations of a solid SMB that provides real value to its customers.

When your SMB is clearly surviving and thriving in the tough private sector, government is increasingly reassured that your product or service has value. It has been tested. It has been refined. It has been proven. With this, the seeds of government trust sprout.

Once a level of trust has been established, the risk of doing business with you decreases.

Once your level of risk, or perceived risk, has been lowered, then government is far more likely to consider your product or service.

Once government begins to consider your product or service, then you're much closer to actually winning *regular* government work and riding that unicorn.

Over the years I've spoken to many business people who have told me how frustrating it is to not even get a look in when government departments — local, state or federal — put the call out for work. They've told me how their offering is so fantastic because it does this, that and the other. They've told me how government must be backward not to do business with them. Most of the time, these people haven't been in business long. Most, but not all of the time, they haven't been making any waves in the private sector. Most, but not all, of the time, their offering has a limited track record. It should not surprise them that government hasn't welcomed them to the fold. But it does.

They simply haven't appreciated that when your company has a proven history of growth — or even just stability — in the private sector, the government door begins to inch open.

ABSOLUTE 1

Governments prefer SMBs with **real-world cred**. You need a private-sector track record.

GET IN TOUCH

It's all very well — and very necessary — to dream big. However, if you want the best chance of realising your dreams, the first part of your chase must be plotting, planning and proving yourself.

Once you have scored your real-world runs, then you can evolve your business to go after unicorns.

That's not always easy to do, and I'm happy to offer advice for your specific case. Let's talk via email: government@ thinqlearning.com.au.

ABSOLUTE 2

THE **ONUS IS ON YOU** TO FIND
GOVERNMENT OPPORTUNITIES.
MONITOR GOVERNMENT SITES
DAILY.

CHAPTER NINE

Ask for help

TO HELP SMBs INCREASE their chances of doing business with any level of government, there's one organisation that offers a myriad of support and development programs. This organisation offers a host of workshops, webinars and events designed to strengthen SMBs, boosting their ability to increase revenues in both the public and private sector. This organisation offers investment and funding support to help them get started, grow and thrive. What is this mysterious, all-powerful being that seems to fly in like Superman to help small business succeed?

Ironically, it's the Queensland Government.

And, yes, I know that not all SMBs will agree with this statement.

Before I go on, I feel you, my honoured reader, needs to understand that I have never been employed by any level of the Queensland Government. I have never run for office at any level, and have no plans to. I have not been commissioned by the Queensland Government to include this chapter. I am simply a keen student who's spent a long time deciphering the sometimes mysterious ways of governments in all their forms.

Further, you need to understand that it's in the best interests of any government that its small business sector is strong and growing. Show me a government — I don't care which side of politics they sit on — that doesn't support a resilient and expanding SMB sector and I'll show you a government leading a softening economy. It's a government that is likely to be swiftly and soundly removed from office come election time. The Queensland Government hasn't put all its SMB support programs together on a whim. They know how much SMBs are worth to the state economy.

Here's a few fun facts about Queensland small business that government is keenly aware of. In Queensland:

- Small business contributed close to $113 billion to the economy in 2017/18
- There are more than 400,000 small businesses — this is 20 percent of all small businesses in Australia
- 44 percent of the entire private sector workforce is employed by SMBs
- A calculated 97.4 percent of all businesses are SMBs
- There are, on average, 86 small businesses per 1000 residents.

When looked at as a sector, small business is not small at all: it's extremely big and extremely valuable. It's important that all levels of government provide as much support and assistance as possible to ensure it grows. For its part, the Queensland Government has put in place many initiatives that can really help SMBs. I've spoken to many SMBs about these programs. The feedback is a mixed bag.

Some are aware of a few programs available. Some aren't. None are aware of everything the Queensland Government is doing to help small businesses. A few have benefited directly from grants, mentoring and other assistance. Most have not. Most have never even considered applying. When I question SMBs on why they aren't making the most of state government's help, three common themes arise:

1. Lack of time

Lack of time is a constant challenge for most SMBs. It's a common practice for SMBs to identify the essentials required to run their business and disregard the rest. Often, the challenges of everyday BAU results in 60-plus-hour working weeks for small business owners. Few have the luxury of researching government programs that they might or might not qualify for, then find the time to complete the documentation required to apply for it.

2. Lack of awareness

While the Queensland Government has many programs to help SMBs, the entry points to these programs are not common knowledge. SMBs have so much day-to-day noise in just keeping their company operating and moving forward, that government messaging isn't always heard. Even when it is, the SMB then has to act on it which then creates another problem — see point 1.

3. Professional pride

Many SMBs also have a belief that there's little the government can do to help them. They know their sector. They know their products. They know their markets. They know their customers. They know far more about their sector than a government advisor stuck behind a desk all day ever will. The only help they want from government is to 'reduce red tape'. While I agree government does need to cut a lot of tape, the SMBs that neglect government programs out of what boils down to professional pride are making a big mistake and missing many opportunities to strengthen and grow.

SO MUCH TO CHOOSE FROM

Whether you're a believer or not, governments are big fans of SMBs. Each of the three levels have implemented countless programs to help SMBs form and grow. Below you'll find a relatively comprehensive list of the programs and initiatives available to help support small business.

Start with the **Australian Small Business and Family Enterprise Ombudsman's (ASBFEO) office**. They're an independent advocate for small business owners. They have the legislative powers needed to effectively influence the nation's lawmakers, ensuring legislation and regulations are put in place to help small businesses grow. The ASBFEO office also provides small businesses and family enterprises with assistance should they find themselves involved in a business dispute. URL: https://www.asbfeo.gov.au/

General links for Queensland SMBs

Australian Government Grants and assistance programs
Find grants, funding and support programs from across the Australian Government to help your business grow and succeed.
URL: www.business.gov.au/Grants-and-Programs

Business Queensland
A source of news, programs, events, support tools and services for Queensland SMBs.
URL: www.business.qld.gov.au/

Federal Government Information and Services for Business
A source for Australian Government grants, services and business tools.
URL: www.business.gov.au/

Queensland Government Grants Finder
Search for the most appropriate grant to meet your enterprise and industry needs.
URL: www.grants.services.qld.gov.au/#/

The Biz BUZZ
A joint initiative of RDA Brisbane and the Brisbane West Chamber of Commerce, this is a Facebook feed of government grants, events and other items or opportunities relevant to SMBs in South East Queensland.
URL: www.facebook.com/The.BUZZ.Qld/

Strategic support and development programs and services

Australian Small Business Advisory Services (ASBAS) Digital Solutions

A joint effort between Business Station and RDA Brisbane, this is a low-cost, high-quality digital advisory services to SMBs across Queensland. Includes one-on-one consultations, workshops and news updates.

URL: https://asbas.rdabrisbane.org.au/about-asbas

Build a Better Business Program

Delivered by TAFE Small Business Solutions, this program offers a series of workshops and one-on-one mentoring sessions with mentors who are highly successful business executives.

Notes: Cost is $455 to eligible applicants (valued at $2,390 but government subsidised). Eligibility criteria apply.

URL: https://business.tafeqld.edu.au/workshops/view/build-better-business-workshop

Mentoring for Growth (M4G)

Offers access to expert business mentors who provide insights, options and suggestions relating to specific enterprise challenges and opportunities. M4G is delivered through both panel and chat formats and can be conducted via face-to-face and online meetings. Notes: No cost. Eligibility criteria apply.

URL: www.business.qld.gov.au/running-business/growing-business/business-mentoring/mentoring-growth

TAFE Small Business Solutions

Helps business owners and managers to create ideal business model solutions. Delivered through a series of workshops and one-on-one mentoring, the teachers work with you to figure out the ideal solution for your SMB.

URL: https://tafeqld.edu.au/information-for/employers/small-business-solutions.html

Workshops, webinars, events and readings

Business Queensland Events Calendar
Find and register for business and industry workshops, webinars, forums and events across Queensland.
URL: www.business.qld.gov.au/running-business/support-assistance/events

Entrepreneurs Guide
A freely downloadable guide from the Australian Stock Exchange that gives a logical approach to starting, growing and exiting an innovation-driven enterprise.
URL: www.caxtoninc.com/

EXPRESSWAY Network forum
A forum for Queensland business managers and innovation leaders from all industries, sectors, regions and business stages. The monthly forum events are a venue for networking, collaboration, education and investment. Notes: No cost to join or attend forums, but eligibility criteria apply.
URL: www.linkedin.com/groups/6502092/

EXPRESSWAY Network on LinkedIn group
An online group that brings together innovative business managers so they can share articles, learn about support programs for innovative enterprises and keep in touch. Notes: No cost, but eligibility criteria apply.
URL: www.linkedin.com/groups/6502092/

Running a Business
Vital information to help you run your business in Queensland.
URL: www.business.qld.gov.au/running-business

Starting a Business Guide
An Australian Government guide to each step of starting a business.
URL: www.business.gov.au/Guide/Starting

Starting a Business in Queensland
A service on what you need to know to help you get into business in Queensland.

URL: www.business.qld.gov.au/starting-business

Investment and funding programs and support

Grant writing guide
This freely downloadable guide offers advice about how to write grant applications.

URL: https://teq.queensland.com/industry-resources/how-to-guides/obtaining-a-grant

Mentoring for Investment (M4I)
A program that surrounds enterprises that are approaching investment readiness with finance investment industry mentors. Notes: Part of Mentoring for Growth. No cost, but eligibility criteria apply.

URL: www.business.qld.gov.au/running-business/growing-business/business-mentoring/mentoring-growth

Startup and innovation programs and support

ABN Lookup
Search for business names and registrations.

URL: https://abr.business.gov.au/

Australian Business Licence and Information Service (ABLIS)
Find information about licences you may need for your business.

URL: https://ablis.business.gov.au/

Australian Business Registration
An online service where you can register an Australian Business Number (ABN), Australian Company Number (ACN), a business name and so on.

URL: https://register.business.gov.au/registration/type

The Office of the Queensland Chief Entrepreneur

An initiative that supports the development of the startup ecosystem and entrepreneurship in general across Queensland.

URL: www.chiefentrepreneur.qld.gov.au/who-we-are

The Precinct (Brisbane)

An initiative that brings together Queensland startups, incubators, investors and mentors together to help foster collaboration and build an entrepreneurial culture.

URL: https://advance.qld.gov.au/entrepreneurs-startups/the-precinct.aspx

Government tendering and procurement programs and support

AusTender

A centralised publication of Australian Government business opportunities, annual procurement plans and contracts awarded.

URL: www.tenders.gov.au

Local Buy

A service for the Local Government Association Queensland (LGAQ) common-use procurement arrangements for councils and local Government authorities.

URL: www.localbuy.net.au/

Local Government Tenderbox

The online tendering portal of choice for many Queensland local-governments, statutory bodies and other public sector entities.

URL: www.lgtenderbox.com.au/welcome

QTenders

A site that addresses tendering for Queensland Government contracts.

URL: qtenders.hpw.qld.gov.au/qtenders/

Queensland Contracts Directory and Queensland Government contracts directory–awarded contracts
The Queensland Government regularly publishes details of contracts over $10,000 it has awarded on these sites.
URLs: http://qcd.hpw.qld.gov.au/Pages/AwardedContracts.aspx and www.data.qld.gov.au/dataset/queensland-government-contracts-directory-awarded-contracts

Queensland Digital Projects Dashboard
A review of all current major digital projects for improving service delivery to Queenslanders.
URL: www.qld.gov.au/digitalprojectsdashboard

Queensland First
A Queensland Government procurement strategy that gives priority to local businesses with a weighting of up to 30 percent when awarding work.
URL: www.hpw.qld.gov.au/Procurement/ProcurementStrategy/Resources/Pages/default.aspx

Employment and jobs programs and support

Australian Apprenticeships Incentives Program
Financial incentives to eligible employers of Australian apprentices. Note: Eligibility criteria apply.
URL: https://www.australianapprenticeships.gov.au/programs/incentives
Australian Government Wage Subsidies — Information on financial incentives to help eligible businesses hire new staff on a full time, part-time, casual, apprenticeship or traineeship basis. Note: Eligibility criteria apply.
URL: https://www.employment.gov.au/wage-subsidies

Back To Work Employer Support Payments
The Queensland Government offers payments of up to $15,000 to hire eligible unemployed jobseekers in regional Queensland or

parts of South East Queensland that are experiencing significant labour market challenges. Note: Eligibility criteria apply.

URL: https://backtowork.initiatives.qld.gov.au/for-employers/employer-support-payment/

Back To Work Youth Boost Employer Support Payment
The Queensland Government offers payments of up to $20,000 to hire an unemployed jobseeker, aged between 15 and 24, in regional Queensland or parts of South East Queensland that are experiencing significant labour market challenges. Note: Eligibility criteria apply.

URL: https://backtowork.initiatives.qld.gov.au/for-employers/youth-boost-payment/

Workplace health and safety programs and support

WorkCover Queensland Small Business Program
A program designed to help small Queensland businesses to access free work health and safety advisory services. No Cost.

URL: https://www.worksafe.qld.gov.au/injury-prevention-safety/small-business

ALL ABOARD THE INNOVATION TRAIN

As well as the above programs, the Queensland government also offers many other programs for companies defined as "innovators". The government defines these in one of two families:

1. The business develops new-to-world business models, products or services for scalable commercialisation.
2. The business creates or adopts an innovative product or process solution that results in internal efficiencies or productivity increases.

Grouped under the Advance Queensland banner, a selection of the Queensland Government's innovation programs and bodies include:

Advance Queensland Newsletter
Find the latest news and information about support programs, events and grants available to Queensland researchers, innovators, enterprises and industries.
URL: https://advance.qld.gov.au/advance-queensland-enewsletter

Innovation Journey
This brochure provides a great snapshot of the Queensland and Australian Government programs available to support innovators and innovative small to medium enterprises. Save it in your browser favourites so that you are always accessing the most recent version.
URL: https://www.publications.qld.gov.au/dataset/innovation-journey

Innovate Queensland
Workshops and webinars that help innovative Queensland SMBs to strategise, network, commercialise and grow.
URL: https://advance.qld.gov.au/entrepreneurs-and-startups-small-business/innovate-queensland

Innovate Queensland Forum
A LinkedIn resource where Queensland entrepreneurs and business leaders share news, events, articles, experiences, opinions and success stories.
URL: https://www.innovateqld.com/iq-forum/

Innovate Queensland YouTube
An archive of past video webinars on a range of innovation topics.
URL: https://www.youtube.com/channel/UCk5VVApJGAntq OswPToj9Bg

My Innovation Advisor services
Independent and objective consultation towards commercial-isation strategies for innovative ideas. Notes: No cost, eligibility criteria apply.
URL: https://www.innovateqld.com/mia/

Small Business Innovation Research (SBIR)
Funding for innovators to develop and test new, commercially viable solutions to complex Queensland Government challenges.
URL: https://advance.qld.gov.au/entrepreneurs-and-startups-industry-small-business/small-business-innovation-research

SparkPlug
An avenue by which Queensland startups and SMBs can pitch new solutions to Queensland Government decision makers.
URL: https://advance.qld.gov.au/sparkplug

Programs will end, contracts expire, changes happen. It's always good practice to regularly visit the many government landing pages to see what is still available. For a complete and up-to-date list, go to www.thinqlearning.com.au/governmenthelp. It's not an exhaustive list.

GRANTS ARE GREAT

Government grants are another way SMBs can secure much-needed growth funding. Grants are awarded across a myriad of industries, yet few SMBs take the time to look into which grants are available and suitable for them.

Most SMBs point to three main factors that put them off dipping their toes into grant waters. As it happens, these three reasons are also blockers for SMBs doing other things outside of their BAU:

1. **Time:** Grants certainly take time to complete and submit.

2. **Expertise:** Knowing how to write a good grant or tender application is a rare skill. Some grants are straight-forward; some are complex. Polished applications clearly stand out and increase your chances of being awarded. Many SMBs feel they don't have the knowledge or skills to make a solid grant submission.
3. **Money:** There are many companies that will compile grant applications for you. While none of them guarantee success, all charge a hefty sum. SMBs don't often have cash lying around to blow on grant application expertise.

Where to start

The government-grant puzzle can be navigated a little easier by monitoring grant landing pages on a regular basis. You'll need to familiarise yourself with the main government landing pages, then set a weekly or monthly task to go through these sites.

Because new grants often open and close in a short timeframe, you need to be on top of things to take advantage when a grant opens that aligns with your business. Should you decide to apply, be prepared to put some time and effort into your response. There is real cash available here, so a professional and well-thought-out application will give you the best chance of success — even on small grants.

As grants are effectively taxpayer funded, be sure to provide strong justification on why your company should be considered for any grant funds, as well as who will benefit and how.

The Queensland Government's **Funding, grants and resources** page links to grants in four categories: Queensland Government grants, Australian Government grants, Local Government grants and 'Other Grants'. URL: https://www.qld.

gov.au/community/community-organisations-volunteering/
funding-grants-resources

As well as this central resource, here are some other avenues through which you can apply for funding and grants.

Community Door
Tools, resources and information to help community organisations operate successfully, including advice on how to apply for funding and starting a community organisation.
URL: https://www.communitydoor.org.au/

Community Grants Hub
Community-based grants administered on behalf of Australian Government departments, agencies and organisations.
URL: https://www.communitygrants.gov.au/

Funding Centre
An information source on grants and fundraising run by Our Community, a social enterprise that provides advice, tools and training for Australia's 600,000 community groups, as well as services for business, government and the general public.
URL: http://www.fundingcentre.com.au/

Philanthropy Australia
The national peak body for philanthropy and a not-for-profit membership organisation.
URL: http://www.philanthropy.org.au/

Tourism Assistance Database
A broad range of information about funding programs.
URL: https://teq.queensland.com/?redirect=www.tq.com.au

Valuing Organisational Improvement and Community Excellence (VOICE)
This website provides management resources designed to help with the day-to-day running of a community organisation. It contains user-friendly information about office administration and management, along with 'how-to' guides, templates and samples on various topics.

URL: https://communitydoor.org.au/organisational-resources/
administration/policies-procedures-and-templates

GENERAL GRANT APPLICATION ADVICE

Okay, so you've found the first government grant that fits nicely into your company's area of expertise. Take a deep breath. Now what? The task seems huge, but the pay-off will help your business through some tricky economic times ahead. The following five points are your next steps. They're not complex in any way, but they are important. So, when you've read them once, read them again. Then go ahead and apply them in your response.

1. **KISS:** Keep it Simple, Stupid. Brevity is the soul of wit. Brevity is also the soul of any grant application. Keep it simple. Keep it succinct. Keep it as brief as you can, without compromising the application.

2. **Use local suppliers:** If goods or services need to be purchased to fulfil a grant, make it very clear that you'll use local suppliers wherever possible. By doing this you're showing government that if you're awarded the grant, local businesses will directly receive benefits through your engagement with them.

3. **Play to your strengths:** While government won't tell you this, grants are more likely to be awarded to businesses that can show growth, stability and profitability. Governments shy away from risk where they can, so if you have good financials in place, you'll be considered far more favourably than those that don't.

4. **Tell a story:** Everyone loves a good story. Paint a vivid picture of how choosing you will result in many other benefits on top of the grant's objective.

5. **Triple-check you are eligible:** Check, check, and check again that you're 100 percent eligible for the grant. Putting together an application takes time and receiving a letter from government advising you that your application was rejected because you weren't eligible in the first place can be soul destroying.

ABSOLUTE 2

The **onus is on you** to find government opportunities. Monitor government sites **daily**.

GET IN TOUCH

It might all seem bewildering now, but you'll soon learn which are the few channels most suited to your business, your sector and your strategy.

If it's not coming together, send me an email explaining what your business is about and what it is looking for and I'll see if I can help. Message me at: government@thinqlearning. com.au.

ABSOLUTE 3

GOVERNMENTS WILL EXPLAIN
THEIR DECISIONS. WIN OR LOSE,
ALWAYS REQUEST A DEBRIEF.

CHAPTER TEN

Learn by losing

FOR LARGER PIECES OF government work, you will need to spend more time putting together a formal submission. In this, you will need to justify and qualify why your SMB is right for the contract. You will need to produce a presentation that clearly shows why you're the company most capable of fulfilling the brief. You will need to establish and validate why your SMB should be handed the keys.

And you will be unsuccessful.

You'll likely be unsuccessful many times over. However, it's what you do *after* the battle is lost that will either help you scale the government walls and win future opportunities ... or see you meekly turn on your heels and look for a smaller castle to storm.

Excusing the use of 'his', John Dewey summed this up well when he once said: "Failure is instructive. The person who really thinks learns quite as much from his failures as from his successes."

Thomas Edison's most famous invention was the commercially viable lightbulb. He allegedly had over 1000 failures before he created a successful prototype. A reporter once asked him what it felt like to fail 1000 times over. Edison replied, "I didn't fail 1000 times. The lightbulb was an invention with 1000 steps."

Whenever you lose out on a piece of government business, you'll be disappointed. You'll ask yourself what went wrong. You'll consider all the time you put in. You'll question whether to continue the fight to open government revenue streams.

When you ask this question, you face the opportunity to discover why you weren't successful. If you just take one more step right here, the room you enter has the potential to bring you much closer to winning future government business. It's called a debrief, and government usually offers debriefs to all unsuccessful tenderers. Embrace debriefs and you'll be stronger. Ignore them and you will continue to stumble around blindly hoping to one day catch that elusive unicorn.

THE DEBRIEF

Most government agencies offer formal debriefing sessions for companies that have submitted unsuccessful applications for work. The key is you must ask for it. Like you, everyone is busy — including government officials. Government officials won't just contact you after you've lost a piece of work to explain why they chose someone else.

The onus is on you to immediately request a debrief session when you don't win a piece of government business. Go along, listen with an open mind, pay attention and learn — you won't regret it.

The primary goal of these sessions is to give you insight into how you can submit a more competitive bid in future. If executed correctly, debriefs offer meaningful information pertaining to the strengths and weaknesses of your submission. In receiving this information you are getting vital feedback that will make your future submissions that much better.

Most government agencies offer these debrief sessions as part of the overall process. However, if an agency doesn't openly offer a debrief, they must provide one upon request. There are some rules that you must abide by in these meetings. The major rule is that you aren't allowed to discuss, question or compare your submission to the company that was successful. Instead, here are a few good topics to raise in the debrief:

- Some indication in relation to your costs, i.e. are you far too expensive for this piece of work?
- The strengths of your offer
- The weaknesses
- Resource issues or deficiencies
- Issues around aspects of subcontracting, if applicable
- Issues around your experience or qualifications.

The bottom line

Above all else in your debrief session, you must ask: "How did our submission rate against each selection criteria?"

This is the most important thing you can take away. In this situation, knowledge certainly is powerful. You'll learn where you nailed the brief. You'll learn where you crashed and burned. You'll uncover valuable intel that will help you in the future.

Even better, prior to your debrief, send government an outline of what you'd like clarification on. Highlight the question of how you rated against the selection criteria front and centre. This will ensure you get as much as you can from the meeting debrief — and it's just good manners!

Big vs. small

Many government officials have told me that SMBs rarely request debrief sessions. There is, however, one business demographic that often asks to meet with government when they've missed out on a contract. Any ideas who this might be? That's right: Big Business.

Big businesses know the value of government work, and they'll do whatever it takes to increase their chances of securing future work. They'll send impeccably dressed representatives to these debriefs to uncover exactly where their proposals fell over. Price? Capability? Expertise? Accreditations? Over time, they gather intel that helps them hone their submissions and greatly increase their chances of winning future government work.

Why do SMBs rarely use this strategy? Most of the time it's one of three reasons:

1. **Time:** We've already covered how time-poor SMBs owners are. In this situation it usually means they're too busy to request or attend a debrief before the deadline.

2. **Lack of knowledge of government processes:** Many SMBs simply aren't aware that they should request a debrief even if this is not communicated by the government department.
3. **Skepticism:** These are SMBs that mistakenly believe a debrief will only yield a standardised response as read to every business that requests a debrief. While this sometimes happens, the onus of getting useful information out of a debrief is on you.

If you take nothing more away from this chapter, please take this: if, as an SMB, you ever take the time to put together a tender, grant application or proposal to government and you don't win, *always ask for a debrief.*

If you're sitting back now and cursing yourself for not proactively seeking feedback from government, take solace in the fact that you're not on your own. Quite the opposite. This was also a mistake I made many times until I virtually tripped over debriefs and realised their value.

In my early years I lost lots of government contracts and never even considered meeting with the selection committee to find out how I could improve our responses and proposals. In those early years, I didn't even know debriefs existed until one day ...

I'd uncovered a piece of work for a local council which I thought we'd be perfect for. It was almost too good to be true: everything they needed, we could offer — with extras on top. We had a track record. We had capability. We had a great reputation.

I knew our competition well, and I also knew none of them could deliver this service as well as we could. I'd even gone so far as to calculate the revenue for this work, how much profit there'd be and how the business would use that extra cashflow. I confidently put together a detailed response listing all of the reasons why we should be selected to work with the council on this project. I then awaited the good news.

Imagine my surprise when, a few weeks later, I opened an email informing me that the council wouldn't be proceeding with our offer and that they'd selected another provider. I consider myself a pretty calm and reasonable person. Now, at least.

Back then, I hadn't quite developed those qualities.

I was upset. I was angry. I was insulted.

Without really thinking, I picked up the phone and called the council officer who was the main point of contact. I don't recommend calling *any* professional contacts in the sort of mood I was in at the time. If there exists a business version of insanity, I was sailing pretty close to it. Happily, at least on this occasion, it had a positive outcome.

A nice lady picked up the phone and answered with the same introduction as always. I could barely contain my anger as I did the same. I explained that I had received notification that we'd not been selected for the recent works and how this really surprised me because I knew — I just *knew* — that no-one could meet that particular need as well as we could.

There was a pause on the other end of the line. I got the feeling that the lady was deciding whether to offer the same stock-standard response she'd been trained to offer when these types of calls came through. Thankfully, she took pity on me. She explained that she was about to head into a meeting and couldn't talk long, but suggested that I schedule a debrief session.

Without really thinking, I arrogantly replied that "yes, I would like to schedule that because we've been robbed on this one and I want to know why". I'm not proud of my response.

This very patient lady then offered a couple of dates and times. I picked one and ended the call. At the designated time and place I turned up, still smarting from the loss, but in a much better frame of mind than when first informed. Once the pleasantries were out of the way, I explained how I was trying to understand where our submission fell down — what were we missing — what could we do in future to put us in a better place for government to work with.

The Council Rep then spent about 10 minutes explaining several factors which counted against us. The headline acts were as follows:

1. Despite addressing the mandatory requirements well, we'd not outlined any value-adds of note.
2. We lost points because we weren't listed anywhere as a 'government approved' supplier.
3. We were very highly priced.

Now, on their own, none of these factors were deal-breakers. They each simply meant we'd lost a certain number of points. Then, when everything was added up, we hadn't come out on top. This, I could accept. I had something to work with. I understood what the business needed to do to.

We already had a list of value-adds, although I realised I'd not been placing too bright a spotlight on them in our submissions — easy fix. For the government approved listing, I spent about two hours filling in a form, then paid a $60 admin fee — two weeks later a letter came through affirming our 'government approved' status. Another easy fix. Now, it'd been spelt out that we were more expensive than our suppliers. For future bids I knew we'd need to sharpen our pencils a bit more and make us more competitive — a future fix!

REQUEST. A. DEBRIEF. SESSION.

Assuming you have the resilience and fortitude to continue bidding for government work, treat every debrief you have as solving one more piece of the puzzle that is winning government contracts. Treat every debrief as a forum through which you can refine and perfect your proposals. Treat every debrief as a way of drilling down to what government really wants.

You must turn the disappointment of losing the business around. Consider the debrief after a failed submission as a key step that moves you closer to securing regular and profitable government work. Until you do this, you'll constantly be submitting the same or very similar responses for major government contracts. You will offer the same or similar pricing and solutions. And you will receive the same or similar result.

You will lose.

Through debriefs, you'll learn how to win.

ABSOLUTE 3

Governments will explain their decisions. Win or lose, **always request a debrief.**

GET IN TOUCH

You'll never guess which great wise man uttered this immortal truth: "The only time you lose at something is when you don't learn from that experience."

Nice work if you guessed it was Chuck Norris.

He's correct too. And you don't have to go far to find a similar sentiment pop up again and again across history. It's the core message of the previous chapter too.

If you'd like to hear more about how I personally lived it for the 15 years it took me to gain the experience to write this book, just email: government@thinqlearning.com.au.

ABSOLUTE 4

UNCOVER THE ENTIRE PROBLEM
IN ORDER TO POSITION A COMPLETE
SOLUTION.

CHAPTER ELEVEN

An open secret

IF I WERE TO TELL you that there's a simple way for SMBs to directly improve their chances of winning significant government business, would you act on it?

If I were to tell you there's an open and ethical way to gain deeper insights into a government need, above and beyond what's included in the standard government RFQ documents, would you at least investigate it?

If I were to tell you of a way to get regular access to a government official who is likely very close to the RFQ process (and possibly even a member of the panel that chooses the successful supplier), would you reach out to them?

The fact you're reading this book says you'd likely answer yes to at least one of those.

Assuming this is the case, you need to be aware that on every piece of government business that requires organisations to submit an official response, a government official is also appointed. Think back to any formal government requests for work that you've seen. Do you remember seeing contact details for a certain official listed? That's who I am talking about. For the purposes of this section, we're going to call this official Person X.

Person X is available for anyone to contact with questions about the needs or requirements of the piece of work. Person X is usually the first and only point of contact. They almost always have a solid understanding of the product or service that government needs. Often, they are the *actual source* of the request.

Reaching out to Person X via phone or email, you can:

- Ask questions specific to the tender or grant documents
- Seek clarification on particular components noted in the documentation
- Have them elaborate on sections you don't understand
- Further expand on the selection criteria and mandatory requirements.

Person X can provide real value to SMBs looking to get an edge. Even tiny pieces of information you pick up could prove the difference between success and rejection.

ONE EDGE — NOT **THE** EDGE

By nature, humans are drawn to people they like or respect. When I'm about to make any personal purchase over $500, I usually reach out to close friends to ask if they can refer me to someone who's sought a similar service or product in the past. If so, would they recommend them? Because I know and respect my friends, I immediately have a certain degree of trust for any businesses, people, products or services they nominate.

To help open up government revenue streams, SMBs should try to establish a professional relationship with the Person or Persons X listed on the RFQ documentation. Person X is the contact who can facilitate your understanding of the problem. They can shed light on other issues above and beyond the identified need — these are often beneficial when it comes to differentiating your value-adds.

This whole process is about honesty. You are seeking clarification that enables Person X to feel that you truly understand their requirements.

I'll illustrate this another way.

Say my business needs a fridge. I have a $5000 budget and the fridge must be delivered and installed by the end of the month. I wander into Frankie's Fridge Barn. Like a seagull at a hot chip, the salesperson swoops. I tell him what I need. He asks for my budget and I tell him. I also tell him I need it delivered by the end of the month. He asks if we want traditional white or stainless steel? Ice dispenser? I answer.

He then proceeds to show me three fridges that are all priced between $4500 and $5000. The salesperson assures me they can do me a 'special deal' if I purchase in the next 24 hours. I ask for official quotes, collect them and tell him I'll let him know my decision as soon as I can.

I then proceed to my next stop, Frugal Fridges, to compare prices. I enter the store and look around. After a few minutes I'm approached by a pleasant salesperson who asks if she can be of any assistance. I give her the exact same information I gave the seagull at Frankie's Fridge Barn: a $5000 budget and it's needed by the end of the month.

She asks me if it's alright if she asks a few more questions that could help her make recommendations. I say of course.

She proceeds:

- What exactly will this fridge be used for? Is it simply a staff fridge or is it front-of-shop?
- If it's to be used as part of a sales function, do you want customers to be able to see what's in the fridge?
- If so, do you want see-through glass or these fancy new cool jets that mean you don't need a door at all?
- If the fridge is to be used back-of-house, do you really care too much what it looks like? Will it be used mainly for staff lunches and the like? If so, how many staff?
- Will you need freezer functionality as well?

Armed with this information, the salesperson leads me to one fridge that offers all the functionality I need based on my responses and her understanding of my requirements. She explains that it's a bit over my budget, however it does everything I need it to do. I have little trouble in handing over my card and purchasing the fridge based on her recommendation.

I was Person X here and the salesperson at Frugal Fridges engaged me in a way that Frankie's Fridge Barn did not.

MAKE THE CALL!

When bidding for government contracts, successful organisations should follow the playbook of the salesperson from Frugal Fridges. She engaged with Person X to effectively question and clarify what the real problem was. You should do the same — treating government as the fridge shopper. This is powerful as it enables you to offer a far more targeted and insightful submission.

I've spoken to a lot of government officials about this sort of approach. Almost all say they're surprised at how few organisations make any contact with Person X. When a company actually does reach out, they're most often from the bigger organisations that have teams dedicated to winning government work.

SMBs looking to secure government work must do the same. At the very least they'll start building relationships with different government officials. While that might not help them win the business they're currently pursuing, it could help them uncover new opportunities.

Contacting Person X is a simple way to immediately improve your chances of winning significant government business.

ABSOLUTE 4

Uncover the entire problem in order to position a complete solution.

GET IN TOUCH

It's difficult to position yourself for success unless you understand the entire story, and not just a piece of it. If your profiling skills aren't helping you get to the real guts of the problem, let me know and email me at government@ thinqlearning.com.au. I might have some suggestions that could help you.

ABSOLUTE 5

LEARN FROM THE OTHER SIDE OF
THE TABLE. WHEN GOVERNMENT
GIVES APPLICATION ADVICE,
FOLLOW IT.

CHAPTER TWELVE

Straight from the unicorn's mouth

SECURING GOVERNMENT WORK isn't easy. Yes, I'm repeating myself, but it's important you don't fall into the snowflake trap of trusting the misguided mantra of "you can do anything if you just put your mind to it".

Sorry if this is news to you, but that's complete rubbish. It always blows my mind when I hear people sing from that hymn sheet. I've spent countless hours trying to discover if there was a secret sauce, and, if there was, how I could replicate that formula to win future government work.

It took me years to understand that there's no one path that always leads to government revenue. Sure, it'd be nice if there was such a yellow brick road to skip along while you reach out casually and pluck whichever pieces of government work you desire. Maybe there is one in the Land of Oz, but we're in Aus — and there's no yellow brick road here.

While government procurement and process policy may read that the best conforming offer will always win the business, so long as humans are involved, this won't always be the case. A lot of factors have to be in your favour — and at the right time — for you to be accepted and welcomed into the government fold as a preferred and trusted supplier.

This book is my way of giving you — an SMB owner, manager or BDM — some insights into the process and the benefit of my own chequered experiences. If I'd read this book and been able to apply the 6 Rules and 9 Absolutes way back when I first started trying to partner with government, I would've been more successful, and in a much shorter timeframe.

So, I'll say it again, these are *my* Rules and Absolutes. These are not *the* Rules and Absolutes.

Over the years, I've had hundreds of conversations with government officials. At one stage or another I've asked most of them for their take on: a) what mistakes they see SMBs making in bidding for work; and b) what it takes to work with government. This next section summarises the common themes.

Incorrect formatting

Official government work requests usually come with a clear directive to respond in a uniform format. It's a pretty simple request, really. They're asking for you to send your submission back in a predetermined way. This helps streamline many things, but its main purpose is to give selection panels a baseline to compare different responses.

I can't tell you how many government representatives have expressed to me their astonishment at how often responses are received in a completely different format from the one requested. Most of the time this alone gets them immediately thrown into the "Dear John/Jane" pile. You could have the most perfect, brilliant and cost-effective solution to the problem, but government won't look past page one if the format is different from that requested.

So, if government requests a style or templated response, make sure you follow it. Don't get fancy or creative, just use the designated format guide and you'll at least ensure your response is considered.

Emphasis on the extras

When government goes to market to see if someone can supply them with goods or services, don't assume that's the only thing they're looking for. In fact, assume the exact opposite. Frame your response to not just solve the problem outlined in the official documentation, but also clearly outline any extra value-adds that you bring to the table. Sometimes, it's a case of they don't know what they don't know.

Let's say they have a problem which they believe five big, bad, multi-purpose printers will fix. Company A goes in and says "here's that big, bad printer and here's how much it'll cost, plus servicing".

Company B presents the same or similar printer, with the same or similar costs and servicing. However, Company B also includes a piece of software that automatically adjusts the printer toner so when a job is printed for internal use only, it prints at a lower quality and uses far less ink. When a print is required for external use, it recalibrates to produce a higher quality finish. Based on an estimated usage (uncovered by asking the government designated contact, see Chapter 11 for a discussion of this), this will save the department upwards of $7000 per year.

Who do you think has the advantage, A or B?

It's value-adds like this that government gravitates towards, and not just because they offer a 'something for nothing' bonus (although that's very appealing). By creating extra value propositions, you allow government to solve multiple problems with one solution — and those can be problems they didn't know they had when they went to market.

Finally, value-adds like this give government a chance to showcase their capability and prudence when spending the public purse. Businesses that highlight the extra benefits their solution offers really set themselves apart. When offered similar products or services at similar prices, government will almost always select the company that puts the most value-adds on the table.

Tread carefully, though. Government purchasing officials are taught to analyse value-adds thoroughly. It's important that any value-adds you put forward are real and offer tangible benefits. If they don't, or it's unclear of their real worth, then you run the risk of damaging your credibility and brand and, ultimately, your chances of winning government work.

BONUS POINTS!

Beyond the basic mistakes and value adds, government usually also has a number of incentives to offer companies that qualify for bonus points before their submission is even opened. Unfortunately, many SMBs aren't aware of them or don't believe they qualify.

For example, the Queensland Government offers the following:

Local benefits test

This is a big one ... if you qualify. SMBs can receive up to a 30 percent weighting under the Local benefits test. Unfortunately, large businesses can also qualify for this, and they know it. It's important to note here that the origins of the supplier don't really matter. The true test is the benefits that a supplier can offer the local area. So, a supplier outside the local area

can offer local benefits by employing locals and using local businesses to supply when and as required. Of course, while capability and price remain crucial, the local benefits test considers more factors, including:

- Stimulating employment (particularly in regional areas)
- Socioeconomic development
- Supporting local social objectives.

If you provide evidence on how your work will pass the local benefits test, your submission has an immediate and significant advantage over companies who cannot. Surprisingly, a lot of SMBs are completely unaware of the local benefits test. In future, always look for ways you can have this applied to any government request for work that you're considering.

The SMB boost

Governments regularly introduce schemes to help SMBs win more business. Take the ICT SME Participation Scheme. It was enacted by the Queensland Government to help SMBs access and win government business relating to information and communication technology. The boost it gives SMBs is a good example of how schemes like this work.

Under the scheme, if a formal approach to market is made through a complete tender process, then SMBs receive an immediate advantage over larger companies. During the offer-evaluation stage, government must give SMBs a 10 percent points boost. If they don't qualify as an SMB, they get zero for that section of the evaluation criteria. There's no in-between — it's all or nothing. And a handy head start. (Note: government considers organisations with between one and 199 employees to be SMBs.)

Now here's something you might not expect. Many government officials have explained to me that a lot of small businesses applying for government work, don't even indicate that they're a small business. This means they miss out on the free bonus 10 percent! At first, I couldn't get my head around this. It took me several conversations with small business owners before I began to understand why they'd neglect to inform government that they are indeed part of the SMB community.

There's a general perception that government prefers to work with enterprise-level businesses because companies that size offer more security should things not go as planned. Hence by not standing up and announcing to government that they're a small business, they think they're removing a perception of risk from their submission. While I can see where the origins of this come from, sometimes I think it's Big Business that has planted and encouraged this misdirected belief. You should take absolutely no notice of it.

Understand that a government that isn't supporting and implementing serious initiatives to encourage, help and grow small business, is a government getting ready to warm the Opposition benches. Almost half of the entire workforce in Queensland's private sector (that's 900,000+ workers *and* voters) are employed by small business. The state government is acutely aware of this.

So, take the 10 percent. Heck, take any extra percentage points on offer. It's hard enough for SMBs to compete with Big Business without meekly handing back advantages on offer. Look at it another way, by not taking the 10 percent you are effectively handing it to your larger competitors.

Diversity in the workplace

If you have an employee with Indigenous heritage, you'll receive anywhere between a five percent and 10 percent increase on any formal application for Queensland Government business. Many SMBs are unaware of their employees' backgrounds, so make it a point to find out. Again, any extra advantage available must be taken.

Note: this also applies to collaborative bids. So, if you're part of a submission from a group of businesses and you don't qualify for this, be sure to check if any of your partners do. If so, ensure this is made clear when responding. Let's say you don't currently have any employees of Indigenous background but that one of your suppliers does. If this supplier will be involved in your solution, there's a good chance your application will qualify for the extra 5–10 percent. Again, ensure you provide evidence.

Doing the numbers

Many governments use a scoring method from one to five when assessing criteria responses. Being aware of this can help you because it gives you insight into how your submission will be graded against each evaluation criteria.

Typically, it goes like this:

1. Major non-compliance with requirements
2. Doesn't meet requirements, but may be adaptable
3. Meets requirements, except for minor aspects
4. Meets requirements
5. Exceeds requirements.

Fives are fantastic. As for ones: you don't want any of them.

Once you have drafted a response for a piece of government work, I recommend you have a third party go through it and offer their own scores against each selection criteria. Even more powerful is having someone who's been on government selection panels critique it. (They're not easy to find, though.) Before you go through the feedback, do the exact same exercise yourself. Like the good citizens of Troy who woke up one morning to a big timber horse, you'll be surprised at what you find.

In most cases, your scores will be one or two points higher than the person you asked to critique your response. Look closely at the differences. Identify areas of improvement. At the very least, consider making some changes.

Government officials tell me that threes are often the highest scores they award across all competing bids. And, while ones and twos are common, fours and fives are rarely awarded. Think how powerful it would be if your response to a selection criteria simply 'met the requirements'. If you can do that, you receive a four and get an immediate advantage over most, if not all, of your competition.

If you go one step further to 'exceed requirements', you're in rare air indeed. Provide evidence you deserve a five and watch the government doors open and welcome you warmly.

Evidence, my dear Watson!

Offering the benefits of your solution without backing it up with evidence is a mistake that many organisations make. Yes, I've been guilty of this many times over.

If you can't offer up some real-world examples of how said benefit has been applied and what some outcomes were, then you're effectively relying on government to take your word for it. Take a moment now to think again about how government perceives risk. You'll quickly see why making a claim without providing evidence is not going to work out too well.

If you can't substantiate every response you make to a selection criteria, you need to ask yourself why not? On some occasions there may be a valid reason. If so, I strongly recommend you're upfront and include that in your response. Not being able to demonstrate real-world application isn't a deal-breaker a lot of the time, but it certainly won't help you get fours and fives.

Companies that offer clear evidence have a distinct advantage over those that don't or can't. They're able to show reports, data, statistics and testimonies that outline the proven savings and benefits government will receive if they select that business for the contract! Evidence is extremely powerful when bidding for government work. Know that if you can't offer any evidence for any of the evaluation criteria, you should probably reconsider submitting any response.

Position government strategy front and centre

Across all levels of government, most departments have formal and well-defined strategic plans and/or policies. Publicly available, these essentially provide a transparent look into the department's overall goals and how it plans to execute its policies.

Further, as part of performance measurement, government departments are internally assessed as to how they've performed against the overall strategic plan. Departments that have met or exceeded their strategic objectives can receive incentives in the form of staff promotions, increased budgets and headcount relaxations. Departments that haven't ticked their strategic goal boxes are ... well, let's just say they don't often receive glowing internal commendations.

As an example, the Queensland Department of Premier and Cabinet (DPC) currently has four objectives in its 2019–2023 strategic plan. One of these objectives is 'A high-performing workforce'. How is it going to do this? Following is word-for-word from the policy:

A high-performing workforce

Maintain a high-performing and responsive workforce.

Our measures:

- Our employees are positive about their job empowerment, and DPC's organisational innovation, leadership and engagement.

Our strategies:

- Empower our people to perform to their highest level.

- Foster a customer-centric workforce.

- Foster a culture that inspires our people to collaborate, lead at all levels and act to enhance their impact in our organisation.

- Provide efficient and effective business processes and systems.

- Demonstrate effective fiscal management to align services and outcomes to government's priorities.

- Deliver strong governance and risk management including support for whole-of-government risk management.

So, if the DPC released a piece of work and asked the private sector to submit a response, the companies that align their responses with the DPC strategic plan would have a significant advantage over all others that can't or don't. Why? Because the DPC can directly link the private sector solution to its own strategic plan. By doing this, the DPC is providing further evidence that it's actively working towards said plan. Being able to substantiate this with evidence holds immense value to the executive layer of every government department. Aligning each government submission you make to the applicable strategic plans will secure you many bonus points and will make you increasingly more attractive to government.

USE APPENDICES AS EVIDENCE

For years I included anywhere between eight and 15 appendices with every government submission I made. I used appendices to provide all the supplementary information and detail that I thought may not be 100 percent relevant in the main response. If I was sitting on the fence about including a piece, I'd put it as an appendix believing I was "erring on the side of caution". My thought process was that government would go through all the appendices and find value in some things and discard things of no real worth — sort of like a shotgun approach. I was wrong.

If you are including appendices, use them only when necessary and only for supplementary material to evidence already provided in the body of your response. For example, if, in your submission, you note a similar solution that you successfully provided for ABC Unlimited, you'd then refer to Appendix 12: a glowing reference from ABC Unlimited's CEO about the work you performed.

I distinctly remember a government official once saying to me: "If you think it's important, or might be important to us, put in the response — not an appendix!" Sage advice that would have been very handy to have during my early forays into the government puzzle.

DON'T SHARPEN YOUR PENCIL TOO MUCH

One day I received a phone call from the primary contact for a piece of government work that I'd submitted for. I remember it clearly because she said something that I'd not heard before. After thanking me for the submission and letting me know it was in review, she drew my attention to the pricing schedule. She wanted me to clarify a few items.

I thought this was strange because I felt we'd laid everything out pretty clearly. I was really happy they'd called, though. Perhaps the call was a hint that we'd made it through to Round II.

"Is your pricing the best and final offer ... or are you able to sharpen your pencil?" she asked.

Honestly, I wasn't expecting this. As such, I wasn't prepared with an answer. I stumbled around a little and asked her if she could give me 24 hours to crunch some numbers. She agreed and the call ended.

I now faced a dilemma. I knew I was in with a shot of getting the work, but I also felt I was one of at least two or three other businesses they'd be considering. I figured they'd probably made the same 'pencil sharpening' call to them.

Having already provided pretty good rates that I felt were competitive, there was still a little fat left in it for my company. I chewed on the situation a while. It didn't sit well with me, but I adjusted my pricing with my 'sharpest pencil' and sent it back to them for review. I believed that if I didn't offer revised pricing and my competition did, then I'd likely be the runner-up. Instead, we won that race.

A few years later I retold this event to a trusted government contact. She proceeded to tell me that this was a standard strategy used by government procurement teams. While I figured this might have been the case, what I didn't know was that when you receive a 'pencil sharpening' call the government has usually already completed their assessment and you're the company that will receive the work. Further, your pricing originally submitted has already been factored into the assessment, so regardless of whether or not you drop your prices further, you're going to get the business. When I dropped my price further, I was effectively lowering my profits unnecessarily.

Beware: this isn't always the case. When two submissions can't be split, then the 'pencil sharpening' strategy is real. However, it's pretty rare that two submissions tick all the same boxes and are equally appealing.

So, when you receive this kind of call, you'll have two options: adjust your price or stand firm and hold your ground. Before deciding, you should do a thorough analysis of your submission. Even better, have someone else do this analysis because they're nowhere near as close to it and may put forward suggestions you'd been blind to.

Once this is completed, if you truly believe your competition can't do what you've put forward at the price you submitted, then call it out. Apologise, and tell them that unfortunately you can't lower your price any further. Explain that a rigorous price analysis was undertaken prior to submission, and, if you're to deliver everything promised at the very high level that your company stands for, then that is what it will cost. On the other hand, if your analysis leaves some doubt as to whether or not your competition can deliver at the same or lower price, then perhaps consider trimming your quote if you can.

Often, government work can be split up into different sections and you can bid for as many as you like. Perhaps then indicate that you could offer a volume discount if you are selected to service *all* of the different sections. The volume allows you to offer a better rate. Just remember that if you get a 'pencil sharpening' call that it's likely you're already in the box seat to win the business.

LEARN FROM YOUR EXPERIENCES

If you can put your hand up to admit you've fallen victim to some or all of these, don't beat yourself up. I've felt your pain. So have many others. Many times over. Learn from it. You're now armed with a list of things to avoid in your future forays into government work.

If you've never made any of these mistakes, then it's a pretty safe bet you've never bid for government work. The fact you've read this far says you're considering doing so. If you do decide to start putting your hand up for government, you have no excuse for making these errors. To ensure this is the case, make a note to re-read this section before you click 'submit' on any government work or grant applications. It might just mean scoring a few extra points — often the difference between winning a lucrative government contract or not.

ABSOLUTE 5

Learn from the other side of the table. When government gives application advice, **follow it**.

GET IN TOUCH

In a way, this chapter was all about learning from my mistakes. I made them all because I had no one to tell me otherwise.

Well, honoured reader, you're in luck: you do have someone telling you otherwise. Of course, the real trick is in applying all this advice in the right way.

So, if you hit any snags, just get in touch. Just email: government@thinqlearning.com.au.

GOVERNMENTS RETURN TO
TRUSTED PARTNERS. AFTER YOU'VE
WON A CONTRACT, **MAKE IT EASY
FOR THEM TO RE-ENGAGE YOU**.

CHAPTER THIRTEEN

We're in!
Now what?

IF YOU FOLLOW *some* of this book's advice, you'll make your business more appealing to government. If you apply *all* of this book's advice, you'll significantly increase your chances of winning government work. If I'd known everything in this book when I first poked into the mysterious government ecosystem, I would have cracked the government nut much quicker. With far less frustration.

Anyway, let's fast-forward and assume that you've been applying the 6 Rules and 9 Absolutes day-to-day. Let's say you receive a wonderful email from a procurement team — it reads something like this:

> Dear John/Jane,
>
> Thank you for submitting your response to supply government with flying cars, RFQ 138746239.
>
> We are pleased to inform you that you have been successful and government would like to engage with you.
>
> The Flying Car Panel would like to request a meeting with you on 21 August 2020 at 10am.
>
> Please reply with your availability.
>
> Sincerely.
>
> The A1 Best Gov Procurement Team

You're pretty happy, right? No. You're much more than happy. I can assure you the excitement as you first read that email will be up there with glorious Grand Final wins followed by the after-party of celebration. It's up there with that feeling you got as a kid waking up on Christmas morning with a tree surrounded by beautifully wrapped presents. It's akin to the rush and thrill as you hit the highway for the first time in your first car.

I know this, because I've received that email. When you welcome the news that you've secured government work in any form, it makes all of the frustrations, rejections, and mistakes a distant memory. You're on cloud nine and rightly so. You deserve to be proud.

From here, many organisations will relax in the knowledge that they've won and they'll fulfill the government requirement within the established timeframe. I'd caution you to take a slightly different approach.

IT'S TIME TO SHINE

For every stage of delivering on government work, have the goal of fulfilling each stage or requirement to an *extraordinary* level. Don't talk — sing. Don't walk — run. Don't try — do.

Here is where you have a government committee giving you an opportunity that can quickly and easily lead to other government business and multiple revenue streams. Just as easily they can turf you back out the door with a candid message not to bother knocking again until you have your house in order. Shine as bright as you can and give government every reason to put your business forward for more work as it comes around.

For obvious reasons I can't really help you with advice on how to make your product or service the best it can be. That said, I can help you stand out from the usual crowd. First, ensure the selection committee knows that you understand what they want and why. Remind them, and repeatedly, that it's your goal to help them succeed. If they know this, they'll help you achieve it. Here's some tips:

1. Nail the brief

There will usually be an initial meeting to discuss the project in more detail: deliverables, timeframes, goals and so on. This meeting is where first impressions are made, so make it count.

I'm going to assume you'll dress the part. Next, go armed with everything you *might* need. If you're unsure, reach out to the nominated contact and ask them what will be required.

Before you arrive, ensure you know your solution almost as well as your kids' birthdays. Better is a bonus.

Have questions of your own. Be sure they're not just filler questions. Make them relevant and follow up with listening statements (which we talked about in Chapter 7) that reinforces to them that you understand. If they ask you questions, don't waffle. Keep your answers to questions succinct and to the point. When presenting, make it relevant to the audience and stay on point. Before leaving, summarise your next steps and thank them for their time.

2. Follow up

For any action points that come out of the session, be sure to follow up on them no later than 24 hours after. Sooner is better.

3. Consistently gather feedback

Throughout the entire project, make it a point to gather feedback from the relevant stakeholders. Some suppliers shy away from this as they're afraid of receiving unflattering feedback. I see little point in burying your head in the sand. I've always believed it's crucial to get both the good and the bad feedback. Look at it this way: if you're not aware of negative (or even average) feedback, then you're ignoring any possibility of improving your offering.

Uncovering areas that can be improved is invaluable to any SMB. Further, when government see you act on that feedback and improve your solution promptly, they'll understand that you're a supplier who listens and acts. This will build trust and endear you further to government.

GO WIDE

So you're in the thick of the contract and things are going well. You're beginning to get to know the relevant government representatives, and they you. You're getting a feel for the lay of the land. Conversations are flowing more freely and you're starting to feel more comfortable while fulfilling the work. Now's the time to start to build a wider network of government officials — the more the merrier. Ask for introductions or proactively offer them yourself. Go wide and far. Use LinkedIn or other sources.

This is your time to build a network that will continue to grow over time. After all, you have a pretty powerful intro in that your company is already servicing a contract. If you fail to build your network now, you'll be solely relying on your immediate government circle to refer you around. This might happen, or it might not. So sing as loud as you can and get the attention of others while you have some good runs on the board.

DEBRIEF. DEBRIEF. DEBRIEF!

We've already covered debriefing for failed submissions in Chapter 10, but you should also request a debrief upon completing any government contract. Your request will be granted and a date and time will be set. Use this meeting to wrap everything up and close off the project.

Even better, if there's an extra something you can offer which might help them in future, consider presenting it at the debrief. They likely won't take you up on it straight away, but you might've planted a seed. A debrief can also uncover some areas that you might need to tighten up or improve. This is always very valuable, because it can help you win more government work in the future.

Lastly, always ask government if they can be a reference, and if you can include this in future offers to other departments. There is absolutely no harm in asking. And what've you got to lose? For years I didn't ask this, believing that government wouldn't agree as it might be construed as showing favouritism. Again, I was very wrong — another alpha mistake.

If you hit a wall here, ask if you'd be able to put together a succinct report or whitepaper on the project deliverables. This can be extremely beneficial to an SMB as it will provide a case-study that will open other government and even private sector doors. It can also act as supporting evidence for future submissions.

Whatever you do, don't miss this step.

Debriefs are gold.

MAINTAIN CONTACT

Once the work has been completed, be sure to maintain semi-regular contact with the government contacts you made during the work. Average businesses maintain radio silence until the next government opportunity rises — this could be months or even years down the track. Don't be average.

Smart companies reach out every 60 to 90 days and remind government that they're still around. Chapter 7 has already gone into detail on how to do this, so I'll just give you an applied example right here.

A while ago, I needed a caterer for some group lunches and mentioned as much to a government contact while in a meeting. She recommended a caterer they use. Reasonably priced and reliable work. Just what I needed.

I asked my contact how she came to know of these great caterers. She wasn't sure exactly, but she said that every month they'd send her a new catering menu. This made it simple and easy to use them when required. I asked how much she'd roughly spend through them every quarter. The figure amazed me. Moral of the story: don't underestimate the value of good flyers and maintaining regular contact!

REPEAT BUSINESS

The hardest part of winning and ensuring future government business begins as soon as you secure that first piece of business, big or small. Your job now is to prove to government that they made the right decision by selecting you. Show them what you're capable of and offer as many extras as you can along the way. Deliver on time and on budget. Make it easy for them to work with you.

They will begin to trust you.

They will begin to like you.

They will begin to see you as a valued partner and not just a random company filling a temporary void.

Of course, you must also carefully consider the potential impact of offering up a sub-par piece of work to government. Know this: they won't always tell you, but should you be branded as an unreliable, untrustworthy or poor-quality partner, then it'll likely be crickets and tumbleweeds when you call out for government business in future.

You might think that providing a poor experience to one government department won't be the end of the world. You might believe there are plenty of other departments out there that you can target. If you truly believe that, you need to reconsider why you're in business in the first place.

So, the point is: keep government happy and you should keep your seat at the table.

ABSOLUTE 6

Governments return to trusted partners. After you've won a contract, **make it easy for them to re-engage you.**

GET IN TOUCH

Should you make a good first impression (and win some government business), you must now live up to it — consistently. So, if you've just been accepted for your first government job or you've just completed it, you're in a pivotal time.

If you'd like a word of support, guidance or back up, just flick me a message outlining the situation. Email is best: government@thinqlearning.com.au.

ABSOLUTE 7

POSITION YOUR RESOURCES WHERE
THEY'LL HAVE THE **GREATEST IMPACT**.

CHAPTER FOURTEEN

Get Steve Smith out!

ONE OF THE MAIN issues facing SMBs — one that sends thousands into administration every year — is cashflow. Rather, *managing* cashflow in a way that: a) suppliers are kept happy with up-to-date payments; and b) employees are paid on time. And, hallelujah, if there's some change left over for the small business owner.

Usually coming in a close second to cashflow is the sheer amount of time that business proprietors feel they must put into the day to day operation of their company (see Chapter 9). Yes, time is the curse of most SMBs, especially in the early years. In order to keep running costs as low as possible and give the business capital to keep trading, small business owners fall into the trap of taking on too many roles — often managing only one or two of them effectively. Head of marketing. Accounts payable. Accounts receivable. IT manager. Operations manager. Customer service officer. Sales manager. Like a chameleon, small business operators frequently adopt many different skins for many different reasons.

Unlike a chameleon, whose genetic makeup lets it morph easily from skin to skin, the regular small business owner isn't equipped for so many key roles. While this book isn't a tome to advise you on how to run your business end-to-end, I will say this: thinking you can do it all yourself is like poking a bear with a toothpick. It's doomed to end badly, and not for the bear.

It's the smart operators who know how to give their company the best chance to not just survive but to prosper. They know it's essential to surround themselves with suppliers and specialists who are as close to experts in their field as they can afford. They know that without this robust group of high-quality professionals adding their experience to the mix, their chances of building a successful empire is close to zero.

Many others who are infinitely more business savvy than myself have published guides advising SMBs on this very same issue, so there's little point in me doing it. Some cracking business books that give clear blueprints on how to do more with less are:

- *The 4-Hour Workweek* by Tim Ferris
- *Deep Work* by Cal Newport
- *The 7 Habits of Highly Effective People* by Steven R Covey
- *Organise Tomorrow Today* by Dr Jason Selk and Tom Bartow
- *15 Secrets Successful People Know About Time Management — The Productivity Habits of 7 Billionaires, 13 Olympic Athletes, 29 Straight-A Students, and 239 Entrepreneurs* by Kevin Kruse

Do yourself a favour, pick two and read them. Rest assured, if you only implement a handful of the strategies laid out, it will be a worthwhile exercise.

So rather than launch into my own SMB management guide, I'm going to assume you're running an SMB and, consciously or not, wearing at least a couple of different hats. This, in turn, demands you spend an excessive and often an unhealthy amount of your life 'in the middle of the business'.

The first thing you have to do is claw back some of that time — if you can do that then you'll gift yourself some space and opportunity to apply the 6 Rules and 9 Absolutes and commence opening government doors.

Regardless, if you take this advice or not, in order to realise government revenues you're going to need a plan ... and, yes, this means you're going to need some time.

THE KNIGHT INSIGHT

I'm a big cricket fan. Late one night I was watching the second test of the 2019 Ashes series being played in England. I remember English commentator Sir Ian Botham (knighted for services to cricket and charity) explaining one of the many cricket strategies that I had no knowledge of. I quickly saw how this strategy — which I'll call the Knight Insight — could help SMBs balance the task of targeting new government revenue streams among all their other pressing concerns. I saw how, if applied to the SMB world, this strategy would guide SMBs to efficiently allocate only the essential resources to begin their government hunt.

At the time Sir Ian made his remarks, the English cricket team were having a really tough time trying to get batsman Steve Smith out. "Tough" is probably a generous word to describe the situation. Almost impossible is closer to the truth. See, Smith's average over his previous 10 innings against England was an unheard of 136 runs. England had tried many tactics to take Smith down — legside field, offside field, everyone close in, everyone spread out on the boundary, short ball barrage, good length marathons. None of it had neutralised him. It was even rumoured that while walking off the field after yet another day of cricket dominated by Steve Smith's bat, one English cricketer asked the groundsman "got any ideas to get him out?".

In theorising about strategies that could bring Smith undone, Sir Ian explained how it was essential that the English captain position only the essential fielders in the exact place which would give his bowlers the best chance to take Smith's wicket. Once those fielders were positioned, he could then go about placing the remaining fielders. What really resonated with me was the strategy of placing three or four fielders exactly where they would have the best chance to make the highly coveted breakthrough.

Small business owners who are time poor and trying to add government revenue to their coffers on top of all their other tasks, should have a serious think about the Knight Insight. Because ...

Most SMBs don't have the budgets to employ a team of government specialists.

Most SMBs don't have the experience to successfully pursue government work themselves.

Most SMBs certainly don't have the time to give an end-to-end government strategy.

But most SMBs do have a few key 'fielders' (that is, resources) they can place in the best possible position to snap up any chance of the desired result.

START SMALL

Your first step of the Knight Insight is to pick just a handful of the Rules or Absolutes. I'd argue that most business professionals have the innate skills and abilities to take three Rules and Absolutes and incorporate them into the daily operation of their business.

Though, again, we come back to time, or lack thereof. The time management and productivity books mentioned earlier will help, or you can investigate organisations that specialise in working with government to see how they can help. Failing that, take a class on time management.

Anyway, the point here is neatly summed up in a quote from leadership expert John C Maxwell: "You'll never change your life until you change something you do daily." Thus, until you apply your selected few Rules and Absolutes, you'll continue to be left out in the cold while Big Business warms it feet by the government fire.

Even in good economic times the failure rate of small businesses sits around 50 percent. Obviously, in tougher times this increases. This is why it's essential that once an SMB has runs on the board in the private sector and starts to eye off public sector work, that it begins structuring its business practices and workloads to make government a strong target market. Big business has been doing this since time began because they know the value of executing a government strategy.

Consider what Sir Ian Botham suggested for the English cricket team as they sought a way to increase their chances of taking Steve Smith's wicket. You, likewise, need a plan to increase your chances of winning government business or grants. So, pick your key fielders or resources and you'll begin the hunt for government business.

Here's an example of a strategy which incorporates four of the Rules and Absolutes and provides a steady ship to sail into government waters.

1. Make government see you

Spend some time going through the many networking events, small business programs, coaching sessions, incubators and training programs. It can be a time-consuming task to find all of them as many sit on sites that you might not expect. Further, sometimes they're out of date. Instead, go to www.thinqlearning.com.au/governmenthelp.

This landing page is updated monthly and is a central place for all of the government programs designed to help small business partner with government. You can streamline the entire process by registering on the landing page, so in future any changes made to those pages you'll be notified. This will let you see what has been added quickly and easily. Once you're on the page, then shortlist the events and programs that:

1. Have relevance to your business
2. Are not going to tax your time unduly
3. Provide clear benefits.

Once you have your shortlist, register for them. Most are either free or have negligible cost. When you attend these events and programs you will begin to meet government officials at different levels. Importantly, they will get to know you and what your business does. The connections you make at these events could be the same people who open the government door for you in the future.

2. Partner, partner, partner

Begin to build a partner network that strengthens your business through providing access to new lead lists with the bonus of making you a more attractive provider to government. Sit down with your team (or by yourself, if you're a sole trader), and:

1. Make a list of companies that *could* complement you by providing your existing customers a value-add. Essentially, these are companies that might be a good joint venture. Don't be shy here. Make note of any company which you think might fit this brief, and also note how your company could benefit their customers
2. Make a list of ideas on co-promotion that would be equally beneficial to both organisations. (JVs don't usually work well if one party does all the heavy lifting.)
3. Prioritise your "Dream Partner Hit List", putting the company that could provide the most value at the top.

Once you've completed this exercise, you'll have a potential partner list that both outlines who you can approach about JVs and can boost your government-business strategy. The next step is picking up the phone to call these businesses and gauge their interest.

If your company has a good reputation and offers real value, you might be surprised how many other SMBs would welcome a JV. Most small businesses don't realise the power of strong, *mutually beneficial* partnerships.

3. Be resilient

Don't give up at the first government rejection you receive. Or the second, third or 10th. Learn as much as you can from each rejection and, over time, your government responses will sharpen. You'll begin to see clear patterns as to what resonates with government and what doesn't.

Any government strategy must include the SMB being as stubborn in the face of repeated rejection as possible. Seek feedback. Demand a debrief if it's not forthcoming. Query said feedback if you don't quite understand. Get answers that will help you improve. And then apply them.

4. Be consistent

The three points above will be enough to put you on the government path, and, if applied correctly, will begin to position your business in a much more attractive light for government. However, the major difference between success and failure is in how *consistent* you are with your chosen strategy.

It could take a long time before you're noticed and welcomed onto a government project. Unless you're lucky, success will only come if you maintain your strategy and remain constant over however long it takes to prise open that door.

USING THE KNIGHT INSIGHT

We opened this chapter talking about the Knight Insight — a strategy for getting out Steve Smith, who is, by some measures, the best batsman of his generation. The insight was that the challenge isn't about cracking a hard nut with one hammer blow, it is, rather, a case of correctly identifying the minor weak spots in the shell ... and then persistently applying the right kind of pressure.

This is how the Knight Insight applies to SMBs hunting government business: it's a hard nut you gradually wedge your way into, not one that yields to single dramatic strategies. So, position your key fielders, maintain the pressure and boost your chances of taking Steve Smith's wicket!

ABSOLUTE 7

Position your resources where they'll have the **greatest impact**.

GET IN TOUCH

Sport really can teach you a lot about how any team can get something difficult done once it knows the 'rules of the game'.

Like test cricket, the pursuit of government work is a game of pressure and patience. With finite resources, a strategy like the Knight Insight — of finding your most likely chances, building tactics around them and then maintaining vigilance — is one of the best.

I'm happy to share specific tips on how you can apply it — just ask. My email is: government@thinqlearning.com.au.

MODERN GOVERNMENT PROCUREMENT AND PAYMENT POLICIES HAVE GREATLY IMPROVED. UNDERSTAND THAT THE HISTORICAL BARRIERS PREVENTING MANY SMBs FROM BIDDING FOR GOVERNMENT BUSINESS ARE NO LONGER WHAT THEY ONCE WERE.

CHAPTER FIFTEEN

It's the government, Jim, but not as we know it ...

REASONS WHY SMBs should *not* invest time or resources into targeting government business often get bandied about, and a few common theories have stuck around for years. A while ago I had a meeting with a small business owner regarding a lead-sharing partnership arrangement. We were discussing various matters when the "Big Three" reasons to stay away from government business reared their ugly heads.

I'd asked 'Bob' (not his real name), the director of this Queensland SMB, which sectors he predominantly targeted. Bob gave me a detailed response, however he failed to mention government as one of his targets. I found this a little strange because I knew for a fact that government has defined problems that his company specialised in solving. They were a logical fit for each other.

"Have you actually made a conscious decision to avoid the government sector?" I asked. "And, if you have, why?!"

To paraphrase, Bob listed the classic "Big Three":

1. Government takes three months to decide on a supplier
2. Government then takes three months or more to finalise and implement the solution
3. Government then takes three months to pay for the work.

It has always surprised me how many times the "rule of three" pops up in different aspects of life. And here they were again! Unlike the perception bias that powers most other "rules of three", Bob was unequivocally spot-on ... 10 to 20 years ago.

Back then, you'd have been a very brave SMB to target government contracts to keep your SMB moving ahead. Unless you had deep pockets or people on the inside willing to swing government work your way (yes, this happened a lot back in the day), then, as an SMB, you needed to think very long and hard before committing to partner with government.

Government business was difficult to find. Government business was difficult to deliver on. Governments were, for the most part, difficult to work with.

That's all changed. And most SMBs don't know it.

GOVERNMENT EVOLUTION

The traditional perception of partnering with government is almost obsolete. A quarter-century ago, I listened to my favorite bands on CDs. At the time, CDs were amazing. Finally, I could skip easily and quickly to whatever songs I liked. CDs were super easy to copy and relatively portable. Scratches were a problem, but so long as you were careful you could avoid that issue. All in all, though, I didn't think anything would overtake the amazing Compact Disk!

Now we carry smartphones everywhere and stream from the cloud. Wherever I go, I have access to all of my favourite tunes. Moreover, I have almost instant access to just about any song ever produced. The music landscape has changed. While it may not all be for the better, there are certainly advantages and vast improvements available with modern technology.

Likewise, the landscape of how the government works with SMBs is now very different from what it was 20 years ago. With so much more data and information available in close to real time, governments are far more aware and better informed than they've ever been.

They know how much SMBs contribute to local economies by stimulating growth and offering employment. They know how much tax SMBs provide all levels of government. They know how many small businesses have grown into immense empires given the right climate. Microsoft, Amazon, Atlassian — they all started off as small businesses. As they grew, they typically employed more people and paid more taxes — both realities that strengthen economies.

Governments of today place a much greater value on SMBs than any before them. I'm not saying governments of yesteryear completely ignored the SMB sector. I'm saying they didn't necessarily offer the level of support and incentives that are available to small businesses today.

Bob's not on his own with his Big Three reasons to avoid government revenue, though. While the theories are based on the way the world was once, not what it is now, I know many SMBs that have also consciously decided not to pursue government work. These SMBs need to take a deep breath and analyse the motivations behind their decision to ignore government as a potential customer, and determine if they're still relevant. Let's also take a closer look into Bob's rationale ...

1. Myth: government takes three months to decide on a supplier

Okay, yes, I've seen this happen. Bob is right and sometimes it does take government three months to decide who they'll partner with. In fact, sometimes it takes longer than three months. However, this is very much the exception, not the rule. Once submissions have been received, the typical government turnaround is two to six weeks. Some might consider that too long. Personally, I feel that's enough time to ensure our taxes are being put to the best use in finding the best supplier with the best value-for-money solution.

Myth 1 also completely ignores another valuable government revenue stream that SMBs can tap: BAU work (which we looked at in Chapter 7). I've been the beneficiary of many $500 to $10,000 invoices signed off by a government official within one or two days. Sometimes within hours. Sales like this are so valuable to SMBs that are faced with the reality of fighting hard for every dollar in an increasing disrupted and highly competitive private sector. SMBs that ignore the government BAU work sector are ignoring revenue that is *very* low-hanging fruit. Sure, it's not always in season, but, once you manage to pick it, it's very sweet to bite into.

The days of governments regularly taking inordinate amounts of time to select suppliers, partners or approve grant applications are long gone. It's time all SMBs realised this.

2. Myth: government then takes three months or more to finalise and implement the solution

Again, a long time ago in a galaxy far, far, away, this was most certainly true. However, this is, for the most part, no longer the case. Technological progress has certainly helped by short-cutting processes as well as enabling far more scrutiny and accountability of Departmental KPIs and project timelines.

There's no question that SMBs are sometimes caught up in a six-month project that was initially slated for three months, and are impacted in many negative ways. However, where once it was a case of "if you wanted the government work, then you take the good with the bad", nowadays there are safety nets in place to ensure suppliers aren't adversely impacted when things don't go smoothly. Anything extra that arises after the scope agreed to is up for negotiation. This acts as some insurance for the SMB when the goalposts are moved.

It's also a fact that government departments of today have more KPIs than at any time in the past. This is the age of government accountability and technology. Combined, they enable more control, oversight and course-correction than ever. Dashboards offer real-time insight on government projects and progression. Integrated systems allow for seamless information and data sharing. Unified communications improve coordination, efficiency and productivity across teams and entire departments.

More than ever, governments around the world are expected to provide real evidence as to the value they're adding to the public that voted them into power. As such, governments are trying now more than ever to ensure budgets are balanced and the public purse is accounted for.

It's never been easier for SMBs to do business with government now that there are more checks and balances in place to ensure small businesses aren't left in vulnerable situations.

3. Myth: government then takes three months to pay for the work

Fact: the only times government took three or more months to pay an invoice for me were due to my company's admin errors. We failed to send an invoice; payment was delayed. We sent the wrong invoice to the wrong person; payment was delayed. We missed the Purchase Order (PO) number; payment was delayed. These are all valid reasons why the payment of invoices dragged out. They were also our fault.

Fortunately, when the invoice was sent to the right person with the correct amount, it was almost always paid within 30 days. I'd estimate about 20 percent of our government invoices were paid inside of *one day* once credit card details were processed. In fact, for small businesses, the Queensland Government has a guaranteed payment policy of 30 days from the receipt of invoice. Yes, you read correctly: guaranteed. Sure, you have to first register your business, but that's a five-minute process.

From experience, I've found that many of the biggest companies in the private sector have much longer payment terms than even the most disorganised government depart-ment. One of Australia's largest businesses in the resource sector refused to do any business with us until we agreed to 60-day payment terms — and that's 60 days from delivery! On occasions, that blew out to, yep, three months ... and more! Accepting this was a really tough call for us. We'd finally had a chance to crack into one of the biggest mining companies in the southern hemisphere, but to do so we had to agree to these beggaring payment terms.

I won't say that government errors never force payment delays on SMBs. However, most of the time when payments are dragged out it is down to supplier errors, and not government. If SMBs get their invoicing right the first time, government accounts are almost always paid more reliably than in the private sector.

OPEN YOUR EYES

If you run an SMB and if the above reasons (or others similar) have led you to opt out of potential government work, you need to pause and determine whether those reasons are still valid. The interface between government and small business really has changed. I'd suggest that most of your reasons not to pursue government work are based on problems that simply don't exist anymore.

Hopefully, you'll soon understand that government *wants* to partner with more SMBs. The roadblock to them achieving this objective is now the SMBs themselves. Big Business will continue to mop up significant chunks of well-paid government work until more SMBs make the decision to actively target government and crack open these new government revenue streams.

Whether you realise it or not, government is ready to do business with SMBs. A big question you need to ask yourself is: is your SMB ready to do business with government?

ABSOLUTE 8

Modern Government Procurement and Payment policies have greatly improved. Understand that the historical barriers preventing many SMBs from bidding for government business are no longer what they once were.

GET IN TOUCH

Through this chapter (and book) I hope you've begun realising that the expectations you have of government might need to be updated.

Our governments of today can't be painted with the same brush as those from earlier eras.

And, if you're having trouble finding a door in, I might have a few ideas that suit your specific business. Send me an email and ask away: government@thinqlearning.com.au.

ABSOLUTE 9

NEVER FORGET RULE NUMBER ONE.

CHAPTER SIXTEEN

Making Small Business Stronger

SO, YOU'RE FOLLOWING the Rules and Absolutes. Your government strategy is becoming more defined. Your business is seeking and receiving valid feedback from government after each rejection. Each new submission is an improvement on the last. While you've not had a win yet, you know you're getting close. You're comfortable with your government strategy and it's not impacted your SMB's day-to-day operations — in fact it's forced you to do more with less. You're on the path and knocking on the door. You understand it's a process that will unfold over time.

Over time, government will come to know your SMB and its strengths and where it provides value. Over time your growing government network will trust you more and more as they see your private sector successes. Over time you'll have positioned your company as a very real and viable partner for government.

WHERE TO FROM HERE?

There's a saying I love: "If you're standing still, you're going backwards." It highlights why it is so important for SMBs to always be looking out for new and innovative ways to improve.

Small businesses must strengthen and develop to the stage they feel confident they can hold their own against Big Business which dominate so many markets. As SMBs become stronger and more stable, the country follows their lead and we'll arrive at a time and place where the failure rate of SMBs is much less than what it is today.

So, in this final section I'm going to share my Top 10 list of what I believe SMBs should consider in order to build their resilience when economic downturns hit. This list is a combination of ideas, technologies, theories and thought bubbles. Take them or leave them. I'm sure a few of them will help fortify the foundations that your business is built upon.

Some of you reading this might already be able to tick off all 10. If so, well done — I'd wager that your business is doing pretty well for itself. If this is you, then my advice to you is simply sit down on an annual or bi-annual basis and determine what changes you can make to enhance your company's makeup.

Note: This list is a snapshot in time and is a by-product of my knowledge and experience up to this day. It will evolve as the world does. For example, there's a good chance that by the time of the next edition of this book is due to go to print, most of the technology I've identified to help SMBs will have been superseded. Conversely, things like 'championing customer service' is something that I expect will remain constant for a long time yet. To stay up to date with this Top 10, go to www.thinqlearning.com.au/smbtop10.

1. CUSTOMER IS KING

If there's one thing that has resonated across the business landscape since time began, it's that customers will largely stay loyal so long as they continue to have remarkable experiences. Go above and beyond whenever you can. Include extra value that your competition can't or won't. Pick up the phone and actually speak to your clients and get first-hand feedback at every opportunity.

All this is pretty standard business practice. You could fill a small library with books on business improvement. However, it's when companies receive negative feedback that you'll truly see how much belief they have in their customer service processes. Many SMBs, consciously or otherwise, choose to hide their head in the sand when undesirable comments surface.

Even before mass internet adoption enabled good and bad news to travel globally in seconds, I always viewed negative feedback as a very real opportunity to secure customers 'for life'. For example, I had a customer service process that I followed every day for 15 years when I worked in education services. Every morning I'd go over our event evaluations forms from the previous day. Whenever I came across something I wasn't happy with, I'd pick up the phone and personally call the customer who had signed off on the event in question.

I'd explain that, based on the feedback listed on the course evaluations, I wasn't happy with how we delivered the day before and we'd be investigating this further. I'd also offer them copies of the evaluations for their own records. For the customer, it was valuable for them to hear this first from me, as opposed to a disgruntled employee complaining to anyone with an ear who'd listen.

After I had explained, I'd politely request that they pass on anything they learned should they investigate. The next day I'd phone them again (or meet in person if need be) and ask them if they learned anything more from their own investigations. On almost every occasion they had very similar things to say, like:

- Overall the feedback from the group was very positive
- One person didn't like … (insert one of many minor issues here)
- The person who made the complaint is a serial offender and very difficult to please.

I was already pretty sure this was the case, but regardless I always followed up. Why? Because my early proactive steps showed the client that we could be trusted. Trust usually takes some time to organically nurture, however negative situations provide an immediate way to prove that our clients' best interests came first.

This was just one method of customer service that ensured companies came back to us. It had the effect of drawing our clients closer and making them more loyal. All of this from a situation that, in the beginning, had the potential to cost us both the customer and other potential clients as negative word of mouth spread.

I know a good number of businesses, as I'm sure you do, who continue to live in a fool's paradise when negative feedback comes calling. Those companies are likely to fail — they simply aren't living in the real world where a bulletproof and process-driven customer strategy is essential for SMBs to survive and thrive.

2. ALWAYS REVIEW

You may already have some sort of customer service policy in place. If so, I'd ask that you sit down with a few other people and roundtable how you can make your customer service experience even stronger and more memorable. I have no doubt you can. You just have to take some time to pull it apart and rebuild it while ensuring the finished product is more robust and customer focused. Further, set an annual meeting on the same subject, and repeat this same exercise. So much can happen in 12 months, so an annual review will help your customer service offering retain currency and continue to add real value.

3. PROCESSES? WHAT PROCESSES?

Many SMBs still have no (or at best only a handful of) business processes. Not surprisingly, many of these same companies also highlight the crazy amount of time they have to invest in running their organisation.

When we talk about business processes, we're going to use this definition from cloud company Appian:

> "A business process is a collection of linked tasks which find their end in the delivery of a service or product to a client. A business process has also been defined as a set of activities and tasks that, once completed, will accomplish an organizational goal. The process must involve clearly defined inputs and a single output. These inputs are made up of all of the factors which contribute (either directly or indirectly) to the added value of a service or product. These factors can be categorized into management processes, operational processes and supporting business processes.
>
> "Management processes govern the operation of a particular organization's system of operation. Operational processes constitute the core business. Supporting processes such as human resources and accounting are put in place to support the core business processes."

Without solid, functional and purposeful processes in place, SMBs are making it that much harder on themselves to realise success. Solid business processes can provide cost-savings, simplify compliance requirements, reinforce and increase customer and staff satisfaction, and reduce risk. These are but a few examples of how strong processes benefit organisations. Show me an SMB that doesn't want to realise these benefits and I'll show you an SMB clinging to the side of a financial cliff.

Business processes aren't just for so-called "Big Business". They're equally important, if not more important, to SMBs trying to survive and grow in what is typically a highly competitive and disruptive business climate.

You bake bread? Applying processes will help grow your business.

You cut hair? Applying processes will help grow your business.

You design websites? Applying processes will help grow your business.

Good business processes aren't a nice-to-have. They're a must-have. It really doesn't matter what your company does: business processes are essential.

If you already have some business processes, then sit down and audit them, preferably with someone you trust who also knows your business. How can they be improved? Can any be sped-up by using new technology? Are there more functions in the business that could benefit from a process?

If you haven't realised the power of good business processes yet, then I'd like you to take a few minutes to identify a part of your business that could benefit from a process. Designing and implementing some business processes into your day-to-day operations will result in many benefits to your small business.

Begin by going to www.thinqlearning.com.au/smbtop10. Here you'll find some things to get you started on the BP journey, as well as some suggestions on software which might help you along the way.

4. FIND YOUR 'KEEPER OF THE BOOKS'

I've investigated this from many sources and, while not all agree on the exact duration, whichever figure you choose it's not good: 90 percent of small business operators spend 15 to 20 hours every week on cashflow management. This includes things like payroll, invoicing, purchasing, etc.

Let's delve into this a little bit deeper. Let's say Bob somehow manages to get two weeks off each year. That leaves 50 weeks he's in the business. Let's take another two weeks for public holidays — 48 weeks left. 48 weeks times 20 hours per week is 960 hours. So, Bob spends, give or take, 960 hours every year actioning financial tasks.

Let's say Bob works, on average, 10 hours per day. We can now uncomfortably predict that Bob — and many others like Bob — spends 96 days every year, on what is often basic and mundane financial duties. Now don't mistake me. I'm not saying these tasks aren't important. They absolutely are. But do you really need to be spending *so much* time on them yourself?

Now, I want you to think about what you'd do if I gave you an extra 96 days in your business every year. How would you spend them? Research and development (R&D)? Perhaps reassess your business processes? Some SEO (Search Engine Optimisation) on your website? Perhaps pick up the phone and expand your partner network? Innovate?

If you haven't done so already, hire a casual bookkeeper. Depending on your company's size and complexity, you might be able to hire a bookkeeper for as little as $150 to $250 per month. $250/month, or roughly $3,000 per year. This gets you about 90 days back into the business, and is a pretty good return on your investment.

Your very own 'Keeper of the Books' will conduct payment of accounts, manage invoices, sort out receipts, process payroll, prepare BAS, report on financial transactions, keep all financial records and keep employee records. And your accountant will also thank you for it.

Further, bookkeepers are far better at doing this than most small business operators. Something that takes you all day, they can do before morning tea. So get a good bookkeeper.

A great place to start is the Institute of Public Accountants — they specialise in helping SMBs. Go to: www.publicaccountants.org.au.

5. DIGITAL DETAIL

SMBs without some form of digital strategy have a future about as bright as a setting sun. However, it's important you understand exactly what I'm referring to when I use the term 'digital strategy'. I'm not referring to digital marketing. Digital Marketing is something most SMBs would claim to use in one form or another, with varying degrees of success. No. A digital strategy is much more than glorified email blasts to a largely unqualified database.

I am referring to a defined digital strategy that spells out your digital goals and how you are going to achieve them. This doesn't need to be a huge report with pages and pages of detail. But SMBs do need a plan that incorporates digital assets because, put simply, customers now use digital mediums far more than any other. That's not likely to change anytime soon.

The challenge many SMBs face is that they're not exactly digital natives. A few might be, but for the most part, the majority are just like me — we know enough to make us sound marginally credible over a dinner-party discussion around SEO. However, ask me to sit down and formally plan, design and implement a digital strategy, rest assured the end result will be a lot of cracked eggs and a nasty-tasting omelette.

A digital strategy is crucial to your SMB and it can't be left to best guesses.

Even if you do feel confident enough to coalesce a digital plan for your own SMB, I'd still counsel you to reconsider. Sure, you know your business better than anyone. You know your market. You know your competition. You know your customers.

Here's the big missing ingredient though: you're not an experienced digital marketer. Your full-time job isn't exploring and implementing digital technologies to help businesses grow. You're nowhere close to being an authority in this highly valuable field.

While it will cost you, I implore you to find a good local company that can develop and realise a digital strategy for you. (In Queensland, I've found Lead Laundry are very good and easy to work with. You can find them at www.leadlaundry. com.au.) Companies like this are built to provide the digital services that modern SMBs need. They'll do everything you can and so much more, and they'll do it faster and more effectively.

Most small businesses won't need a digital strategy partner for much more than three to four hours per week or fortnight. When I first began working with Lead Laundry, from memory I had a budget of $400 per month. Within six months the return I received was much more than $400 per month. An SMB succeeding without a proper digital strategy in place is swimming with both arms tied behind its back. Commit to a strategy, do your research and start speaking with someone who can become your digital strategy arm.

Whether you're looking at implementing a DIY or DFY (Done For You) digital strategy, keep these five key elements front-of-mind when building your digital ecosystem. If implemented effectively, they'll also help make your SMB more attractive to government.

1. Customer Relationship Management (CRM)

This is one of the most important and most undervalued digital tools within your business. Essentially, this is the main database of contact, business, task, pipeline and activity data for your company. It really is the cornerstone on which you should build the rest of your sales and marketing stack. It is the "central point of truth".

A good CRM will allow you to manage your people, deals and key metrics. As with any good dataset, though, it's only as good as the data you input. Therefore, it's critical that your CRM is user-friendly, otherwise your team just won't keep it up to date.

Here are some best-of-breed CRMs you should factor into your considerations:

Hubspot
- ✔ Forever free for unlimited contacts.
- ✔ Ability to integrate marketing, service and sales add-ons for a price
- ✘ Pricey when specced up

Salesforce
- ✔ Completely customisable and integrates with nearly every marketing platform available
- ✘ Implementation takes quite a bit of upfront time and dollar investment.
- ✘ Typically geared to medium organisations

Pipedrive
- ✔ Easy to setup and use
- ✔ Low monthly costs
- ✘ May not have all the enterprise features needed for running larger sales teams

2. Marketing Automation Software

The next tool in any 21st Century SMB's arsenal is a good marketing platform. This will allow you to capture lead information, set up email nurture journeys, build marketing workflows, set up landing pages and forms, and start to fill your CRM with useful data.

It's worth noting there are varying degrees of what constitutes marketing automation and it will depend on what objectives you've set for your business as to the best tool for you. Most will give you the option to try-before-you-buy, so you can typically test a couple of platforms before settling on the right fit. It could also be worth investing in a good marketing consultant or agency to help guide you — this will potentially save you some time and money at the front end.

Some platforms worth investigating:

AutopilotHQ
Integrates with best-in-class third-party platforms
- ✓ Reasonably priced
- ✓ Can scale as you do
- ✓ Excellent journey management for leads
- ✗ Requires quite a bit of time to configure correctly with the rest of your platforms

Hubspot Marketing
- ✓ Complete native integration with a host of features, workflows and integrations out-of-the-box
- ✗ Can be pricey and probably not suitable for large email database numbers

ActiveCampaign
- ✓ Reasonable monthly cost with full lead management
- ✓ Has integrated CRM
- ✗ No native integrations — you'll need to rely on Zapier

3. Social media

This might seem obvious, but you must know where you should be playing in this space based on your customer personas. For example, if you're a B2B construction company, it's probably not worth your while setting up a Snapchat or TikTok account. Again, if you target the Asian market, it could be worth investing in a WeChat or Weibo account.

For the record, you should be on at least three social media platforms. This gives you a solid level of presence. Many businesses are on a lot more and have KPIs for each. Here's a non-comprehensive list of platforms you can try: Facebook, Instagram, Twitter, LinkedIn, YouTube, Pinterest and WeChat.

A helpful tool for checking the availability of usernames that you can claim for your business is https://namechk.com/. You can also check out Hootsuite or Buffer to help you schedule your social media posts.

4. Website

Your website is the forward-facing part of your business, often referred to as your shopfront. Nothing influences the sales cycle of your company more than this. It allows potential customers to review your products, services and pricing, evaluate options in comparison to your competitors and update their buying criteria.

The content of your website must support the business goal for your site. Is its primarily purpose to be a brochure? A sales platform? A booking system? A price list? A reference manual? Given a clear strategic brief, a good copywriter can take the message *you need* your target sector to know and turn it into something *they want* to act on. In Queensland, I've found that Search And Site Authoring (www.searchandsite.com.au) are guns at finding just the right words.

So, unless you can showcase your value proposition and effectively drive a call-to-action, then you're letting potential business go by the wayside. Depending on the type of SMB you run, here are a couple of platforms you can build your website on:

WordPress: Ideal for B2B or corporate sites. Plenty of plugins to add the functionality you need. You will need to have access to the right design and development team to deliver this properly as a reasonable level of know-how is required.

Shopify: Built specifically for eCommerce. If you're exclusively selling products online, this is a great option. Big global brands rely on Shopify and they have an extensive ecosystem to plug in marketing and third-party platforms.

Squarespace/Wix: I've put these drag-n-drop website builders together as they are the leading pair of several simple editing platforms that have low barriers to entry, low ongoing costs and a reasonable level of integration available.

5. Email and calendar

There are really only two options to consider here: Microsoft 365 and Google G Suite. Both are cost effective for SMBs, offer options to scale if you're a large organisation, integrate into just about everything and provide nearly all of the functionality you'll ever need. Even better, new features are added all the time.

It would probably be remiss of me to try to provide a comprehensive breakdown here. Even if I could, you'd probably be confused at the end. Personally, I use Microsoft 365 mainly because my company runs PCs and the platform lets us cover all our Windows licensing, Office products, OneDrive storage and the connected collaboration dashboard of Microsoft Teams.

Final advice on software platforms

It's all too easy to get bogged down in the details. Your research around what is the best toolset for your operations can become a never-ending cycle. So, always remember that implementation is key — done is better than good!

(**Disclaimer:** These recommendations are current as of 2020. There's a good chance the Next Big Thing will supersede them in the near future. This isn't giving you an excuse to not take action, it's just a fact of life in the software world.)

For a current list of best-of breed technology for SMBs, Social platforms, technological platforms and services for you to consider, go to www.thinqlearning.com.au/smbtechnology.

6. HIRE THE RIGHT PEOPLE

Finding, pleasing and keeping the right staff is far easier said than done. I'd say it took me a good eight to 10 years to find the right interviewing process that increased my odds of bringing on a newbie who'd be 'right' for the business. Before then, I'd tried all the techniques I could find that promised perfect new employees: personality tests, fancy questions designed to draw out meaningful responses, overly formal, overly informal — you name it. None seemed to stand out and result in better hires. It still seemed like I was throwing darts blindfolded most of the time.

I had candidates who interviewed well, who convinced me they'd increase the KPIs by 40 percent or who'd performed the exact same role with my competition. Time and again, they fell short. Eventually, I formulated a theory that finding the person with the right skillset wasn't exactly the number one priority. This drew me to the conclusion that finding the right *cultural* fit was the real key to finding new long-term team members. Once I found the right cultural fit, then it was a case of coaching and training the new hire into their role. This is infinitely easier, quicker and more enjoyable.

After deciding on this new philosophy, I went about overhauling my interview process. I took it from a 'capabilities' interview to a 'compatibility' interview. In this kind of interview, whenever I conducted an initial meeting with someone, I'd first take a few minutes to get them comfortable and relaxed. I then explained that the interview we were having was to be two-way. By that, I meant that I wanted them to interview me as much as I would interview them. This usually received bemused expressions. I then made it clear that there would be no smoke or mirrors from me, and that I expected none from them. I'd tell them, warts and all, what it'd be like to work here, as well as what I'd expect from them if they were to be offered a place. I also explained that I encouraged 'conflict' in the workplace. More strange looks.

I'd elaborate, explaining how I loathed talk 'around the water-cooler'. I'd make it clear that if they were hired and had a problem or issue, *anything* at all, they could freely discuss it with the entire team together. We'd agree on a course of action and then move on from there — as a team.

If the interviewee could make the adjustment to their mindset, then pretty quickly the interview would evolve into a frank and friendly conversation. Ultimately, we were really just trying to determine if we liked each other, and, at the same time, if we thought we could work together.

Just as we would say our good-byes, I'd ask them to think about everything we'd discussed — the role, the team, the culture, everything. Then, within 24 hours, to call or email and tell me whether they were still interested in the position and why. This gives a candidate time to think things through and make a cool-headed choice. This also gives *me* time to consider the candidate further. To be honest though, I'd already know if

I wanted them for Interview II within the first 10 to 15 minutes of the initial compatibility interview. Anyway, the candidates would always contact me within 24 hours and thank me for the honesty and transparency. Almost every one asked for the opportunity to join our team.

If I believed they'd be a good fit for us, I'd ask them back for Interview II. Interview II was a bit different as I wouldn't be present. Instead, they'd have 30 to 45 minutes with the entire team. This was their chance to ask anything they wanted without me hovering. How difficult was I to work with? The worst things in the role? The challenges? The hassles? The positives? Commission structures? Everything was fair game. It gave candidates the opportunity to really look under the hood. It allowed real insight into what it was like to be on the team and hear it all from those that are walking the walk.

Crucially, this also gave my team the chance to effectively vet the potential newbie. Further, I always knew the team would answer all questions put to them honestly because they knew the impacts of the wrong hire would be felt directly. The post-Interview II feedback my team gave me was invaluable. If ever I were sitting on the fence about a potential newbie, I'd lean towards the team's recommendation. Most times they were spot-on. Finally, if the stars aligned and we all agreed — and by all, I mean the candidate, the team, and myself — then it was a no-brainer: they were offered the position. Since employing this interview process, our average tenure for a BDM went from 14 months to 33 months. In other roles, it was even higher.

Of course, there's one obvious problem with this 'open book' interview process. If you have, let's say, a poor to average company culture, then it will be exposed in the interview process and will cost you good candidates. If, by some chance, it's not exposed in the interview process, then this is likely because you and your team haven't been completely honest with the potential newbie. They may indeed end up working for you, but once they get a sniff that you've not been completely honest with them, all trust disappears. They'll exit stage left as soon as they find another company to take them on board.

In short, unless you know that your company culture is strong and your team trusts you and the business, do not use the compatibility interview blueprint.

There's a bit more to this interview process than I can put here. If you'd like to discuss any aspect further, don't hesitate to reach out. I know that if you're able to implement the structure well, then your screening of new hires will significantly improve and you'll hire more of the right people who fit into your company and its culture.

7. HEALTHY (AND HAPPY)

Another major problem within today's SMB community is an alarming growth in mental health problems. You don't have to look far to understand why. Long hours, huge responsibilities, mounting pressure, work issues, staff problems — they all form part of the day-to-day for small business operators. It's a heavy load to bear for any one person. Unless mental health struggles are identified early, and then managed with treatment, they'll negatively impact the affected person, the people around them, and the business itself.

I had my own health 'awakening' a few years ago. In hindsight, it probably came pretty close to doing me some real damage. It began when I walked into my doctor's office on October 12, 2010 due to a stubborn and heavy headache. For some reason he took my blood pressure. When you see your doctor's eyebrows raise as they look at a result, it's usually not a good sign. So, high blood pressure it was. That runs in the family, so, while I was a little surprised as I'd no history to-date, I wasn't blown away. My doc then asked me to go up the hall so they could draw some blood and test for 'a few other things'. I obliged and got on with my life as usual.

A few days later, I got a call from the medical centre. My doc wanted me to make an appointment to see him to discuss the results. Now, *this* was interesting. I'd never had my doctor request this of me before. I assumed he wasn't calling me in to congratulate me, a then-35-year-old, on having the physical fitness of a 25-year-old. I figured it wasn't good news. I made the appointment.

Now, you don't know me, but I'm a bit of a fatalist when it comes to my health. And with the real-time research powers of the internet, I like to self-diagnose (please don't do this!). For example, recently I went down to the medical centre to tell my doc I was pretty sure I had Parkinson's due to a few physical issues that I'd noticed. I wanted him to advise me on treatments. Five minutes of basic tests revealed that what I really had was mild carpal tunnel syndrome. So you can appreciate how I was feeling leading up to the 'Big Blood Reveal'.

I arrived on time for my appointment. I sat down, looked him in the eye and asked him to tell it to me straight.

"Tom, if you keep doing what you're doing, in 10 to 15 years you'll be dead."

Well, you could've heard an angel fart. I wasn't expecting the news to be quite that dramatic. I waited for the 'just kidding' part, but it never came. My doc then handed me the printout of the blood test results. He said I could take them home with me, presumably as some sort of macabre memento. At the time, the words and numbers meant nothing to me. Now, very different. My bloods looked like this (summarised for you):

Test: HDL Cholesterol, SERUM

CUMULATIVE LIPID RISK REPORT

Total Cholesterol:	6.8 mmol/L
Triglycerides:	14.3 mmol/L
HDL (protective):	0.9 mmol/L
LDL (atherogenic):	Could not calculate because Triglycerides exceed 4.5 mmol/L
Total/HDL Ratio:	7.6

If you don't know how to read blood work, it's enough to know that these are troubling numbers indeed. How did it get this bad? Well, I was heavily stressed from work and slowly killing myself through increasingly relying on a diet of fast food, and next to no exercise. I resolved to change my ways.

I could spend a long time relating everything that happened from that day forward, but that's a story for another time. All you need to know here is that I completely remodelled my diet. It took a while, but I basically began eating only meat, vegetables and fruit. That's it. My wife joined in too. After 30 days, we both felt wonderful. My energy levels increased. I was far more alert at work. Stress levels dropped. I breezed through my daily workload and started getting home earlier. I was happier and smiling more often and far more easily. So much more relaxed. And sleep! Oh, my sleep was so rested and peaceful.

I was amazed at how much a shitty diet can affect the human body and mind. After a total shift to whole foods, I wasn't quite new person, but I was much improved from the one who presented to my doctor on October 12, 2010. After some time with this new eating regime, I went back to the doc and asked him to run another blood report. First, he took my blood pressure. Again, the raised eyebrows, but this time he followed it by telling my blood pressure was perfect. Next, for the all-important blood test!

I came back a few days later and he sat me down and gave me my new blood report. This time he looked me in the eye and said, "Whatever you're doing to have managed these results, Tom, just keep doing it." The report read like this:

Test: HDL Cholesterol, SERUM

CUMULATIVE LIPID RISK REPORT

Total Cholesterol: 6.1 mmol/L
Triglycerides: 4.3 mmol/L
HDL (protective):   1.37 mmol/L
LDL (atherogenic):   2.79 mmol/L
Total/HDL Ratio: 4.5

To this day, I still have these blood reports on the wall next to my PC screen. They're a constant reminder of how much positive impact a decent diet can have on the mind and body. What's all this got to do with mental health?

Back in 2010, I wasn't diagnosed with a mental health illness, but, thinking back, I have no doubt I had some mental health issues, mainly around avoidance. Over time, I adopted a diet of fast and processed food, combined with an exercise routine that consisted of walking from my desk to the break room in search of biscuits. It just so happened that by cleaning up my diet, I also cleaned up my mind. There's one more change that will help you manage the many daily challenges of SMB life: get a hobby. Seriously.

As you'd have read in Chapter 5, I'd always wanted to learn woodworking skills, but literally couldn't put a nail through plywood without smashing my fingers. When I finally booked myself into a class, every lesson became like therapy to me. I could switch off from the world and just focus on the task at hand (or, in the case of table leg tops, over-focus). The craft is so foreign to me and my 'touch' for woodworking is minimal.

This is actually for the best. It means my concentration levels must be high and I become completely absorbed in what I'm doing. Each week's class is three hours of intense and single-minded attentiveness in which I forget about everything outside the woodshed. You might think I'd walk away from those sessions exhausted. Interestingly, it's the opposite. As I drive back home I feel, well … almost light. Free, sort of. It's difficult to put into words. I'm certainly very happy. And really relaxed. It's a feeling I've not experienced at any other time in my life. I love it.

So, Mr or Ms SMB, I'm pleading with you to take on a hobby. Don't put it off. And when I say hobby, I want you to pick a *new* hobby — not something you did as a kid. You want something completely foreign to you, but that you've always been interested in or admired. Glass blowing. Jewellery making. Leatherwork. Knife forging. Lead lighting. Sewing. A new musical Instrument. Whatever. Personally I think it should be a bit creative and also something you have no current skills in. Reason being that it will help you just to fall into that world at your lessons. It's so easy, then, to lose yourself completely. It'll also help to keep you coming back for more. As you learn new skills and techniques, you'll want to learn more. And more.

I just started a bowl-turning course at the RM School of Woodworking (www.rmschoolofwoodworking.net.au). It's my third course there and I can see myself spending a lot more time there over the next couple of years. Apart from learning new skills and having a great time, I know this hobby helps keep my mind healthy and active. And that is the best defence against mental health illnesses.

8. CHALLENGE EVERYTHING. REGULARLY.

While most SMBs won't admit it, for many, their processes and operations are rooted in the past. What was once considered best practice is now considered archaic.

15 years ago, it was considered good practice to deliver an invoice within two to three days. Now, with the right technology, it's down to two or three seconds.

15 years ago, it was realistic for significant website changes to take three to five days. Now changes can be made in close to real-time.

15 years ago, it was virtually impossible to understand how your customers were interacting with your marketing initiatives. Now, software can report on client interaction within minutes.

For those who can afford it, get an external consultant to come in and audit your business from top to bottom. Your onboarding, digital strategy, sales processes, accounting, operations — everything. The recommendations you'll receive will be enlightening and, often, quite scary. Take it all on board, take a deep breath and identify what changes you can make. Then go ahead and make them. Start with the small ones and work up from there. Every change you make will help build a stronger business.

If you can't afford to bring in an external party to do this, you'll need to DIY. Yes, it's cheaper, but it'll also be much harder. You're close to your business, so taking your blinkers off will be difficult. It's a classic case of not being able to see the forest for the trees. While you might be able to see the details, you'll often miss the larger issues.

It's good business practice to conduct an audit every year or two. If you don't, you'll run the risk of opening up your existing customer-base to your competition. Your new customers will also slow to a trickle when it's just easier, simpler and cheaper to do business with your competitors. Regular reviews will keep your hand on the tiller and keep your SMB from falling behind in the market.

9. NEVER FORGET RECOMMENDATION ONE

Without customers, every SMB is in strife. A detailed and comprehensive customer service strategy is extremely valuable to SMBs. It can not only help you keep regular clients loyal, but will also help you capture negative customer experiences and turn them into positive outcomes.

Today sees reviews positive and negative accelerate out to the market in record time. According to business.com between 67 percent and 90 percent of people look for reviews before they make a purchase. It was also estimated that, in 2017, US$537 billion was lost due to customers switching to different brands after a bad experience. This is one statistic you don't want to be part of.

Perhaps even more challenging is the widely accepted belief that it takes 40 positive reviews or comments to negate the effect of one negative review. Got five negative reviews last quarter? Well, you're going to need around 200 positive reviews, give or take, to dispel them.

I've experienced first hand how difficult it can be to win over new clients from the competition only to only lose them due to a poor customer service strategy. Make your customer experience as magical as it can be. Make it extraordinary and watch your revenues increase. Make it best-of-breed, keep it there and watch the market edge further into your corner.

10. PARTNERS ARE POWERFUL

I've covered this in some detail in Chapter 2, but I believe it's well worth reinforcing for you again. An SMB with a strong partner ecosystem that helps them reach new customers through JVs, affiliate agreements and the like, is far more likely to succeed — especially through rough economic periods.

Partner arrangements have traditionally been neglected by a lot of smaller businesses, and I've always struggled to understand exactly why this is the case.

Partnerships offer paths towards new customer market and segments

Partnerships offer access to a more diverse product mix and better value-adds for your customer base.

Partnerships offer opportunities to entertain and then deliver larger-scale projects that might otherwise be difficult for an SMB to facilitate.

Partnerships not only offer immense value when bidding for government business, they can be as equally powerful in the private sector.

The organisations that already see partnering as an asset and have built a partner network are seeing the benefits of their labour. You, as an SMB, must consider the pros and cons of partnering and conduct an exercise making note of each.

I think you'll find many pros. You'll also find mostly crickets and tumbleweeds in the cons. I'd recommend reading Michael D. Eisner's book *Working Together: Why Great Partnerships Succeed*. It looks into some of the most successful business partnerships and why they were so successful.

Partnering doesn't need to be too complicated. Partnering doesn't need to be overly time-consuming. Partnering doesn't need to be inordinately expensive. If making SMBs stronger were a tree, partnering would be its established and abundant root system. While partnerships won't recession-proof your company, they will provide a much thicker skin when our economy hits difficult waters.

ABSOLUTE 9

Never forget Rule number one.

GET IN TOUCH

I think you've heard enough from me, so I'm going to begin wrapping up. Specific advice for your specific circumstances is beyond any book. However, I'm always willing to hear your story, learn more and help where I can. Feel free to send me an email. I'll be glad to receive it at government@thinqlearning.com.au.

"DO OR DO NOT. **THERE IS NO TRY**."
— YODA

CHAPTER SEVENTEEN

Goodbye for now

CONGRATULATIONS ON REACHING the final chapter! You are so close to the end and it would be a travesty if you didn't finish. As you've read this far, it's relatively safe for me to conclude that you're at the decision point. You're either close to enacting a strategy whose goal is riding the biggest unicorn … or you've decided it's not the way you want your SMB to roll.

If winning government business was easy everyone would be doing it. It's not. If that message hasn't got through to you by now, then perhaps I need to revise some of this content.

Small business has a horrendous failure rate in Australia, and it's time for this to change. I emphatically believe that if SMBs knew how to improve their chances of winning government work, the SMB failure rate would drop. Big Business has traditionally been a major beneficiary of the public purse. Change is well overdue. SMBs can now compete on an equal footing with their largest competitors. They can do this effectively by incorporating the 6 Rules and 9 Absolutes into their daily operations.

With a sound strategy, consistent message, a valuable offering and the occasional bit of luck, SMBs have all the tools available to win profitable government contracts that will solidify and strengthen their financial positions, and benefit entire communities.

I've changed my thinking over the course of the last 20 years or so. Where I once wanted to command a Big Business and lead it on to dominate its market over all others, now I want nothing of the sort. In fact, I now loathe that mindset. My professional life is now about helping SMBs become stronger, more resilient and prosperous. Guiding them into government revenue streams is one very powerful way this can be achieved.

By taking this path, I know I'll have a far more meaningful and positive impact on this fantastic country of ours. And, happily, this is something that I enjoy so much that it doesn't even seem like work — not sure how many people get to hand-on-heart admit that!

Lastly, I just wanted to thank you for taking the time to read this book. I'm not a trained writer and I know any critics reading will pick this apart, but I've really enjoyed putting pen to paper. I'm sure a more gifted writer could make this message sing and inspire the readers to change the world immediately. I know I can't boast the same, but even so, I'm proud of what I've put together for our SMB family.

This is the start of a new journey in my life — one I'm already enjoying immensely. Providing the tools and resources to make SMBs tougher, more versatile and responsive will only result in meaningful outcomes for all of us.

"DO OR DO NOT. THERE IS NO TRY." — YODA

Yes, applying for government work can seem daunting — especially if you've never done it before. But look at it this way: if you don't bid for government work, some of your direct competitors will. They have been and will continue to apply for government contracts. They lose some. They win some. Every time they submit, they refine and polish their approach.

If you continue to dismiss government business, you're essentially handing over decent chunks of revenue directly to your competition. It's an alpha mistake. Your competition will strengthen as they cement public and private avenues of revenue. You will continue to play in the space you feel comfortable. The question is: will your space be big enough to sustain you through extended periods of difficult trade?

Should you make the decision to look at government work as opportunities to expand and fortify your business, you will have commenced a journey that could grow your business to levels previously not imagined.

It won't be an easy journey.

Many times you will feel like throwing it in and going back to the old ways. You will be rejected — likely many times. You will get disheartened. You will often question whether any of your government work will ever pay off.

Then one day you'll get that call, and that government gate that had always remained steadfastly shut, will open a little for you, and you'll take your first tentative steps through the opening. Cue triumphant music.

Goodbye for now! I wish you all the success in future.

KEEP IN TOUCH

To keep up to date with my blog, you can subscribe at:
www.thinqlearning.com.au/government

To get an online report on your SMB's readiness to win government work, go to:
www.thinqlearning.com.au/govpulsecheck

To stay informed about government developments, works and the like, subscribe to my newsletter:
www.thinqlearning.com.au/government

To reach me direct, use the contact details below:
- LinkedIn: linkedin.com/company/thinqlearning
- Email address: government@thinqlearning.com.au
- Company switch: (07) 3040 5811
- Facebook: facebook.com/thinqlearning
- Twitter: twitter.com/thinqlearning

If you enjoyed this book and know someone who might benefit from reading it, please pass it along or invite them to visit www.thinqlearning.com.au/government.

"AUSTRALIA IS A NATION OF SMALL BUSINESSES — **THE ENGINE ROOM OF THE ECONOMY**."
— KATE CARNELL

The 6 Rules and 9 Absolutes for winning Government business

THE 6 RULES

SMBs that follow these 6 Rules will capture more opportunities to win new revenue through government work.

1 Partners must be actively sought and managed — always within a win:win framework.

2 Build relationships with and learn from peers who already work with government.

3 Follow the axiom that "mandatory doesn't always mean mandatory".

4 Prioritise criteria according to their weighting.

5 Stay the course. You will not succeed with your first attempt.

6 It all starts with a phone call.

THE 9 ABSOLUTES

1 Governments prefer SMBs with real-world cred. You need a private-sector track record.

2 The onus is on you to find government opportunities. Monitor government sites daily.

3 Governments will explain their decisions. Win or lose, always request a debrief.

4 Uncover the entire problem in order to position a complete solution.

5 Learn from the other side of the table. When government gives application advice, follow it.

6 Governments return to trusted partners. After you've won a contract, make it easy for government to re-engage you.

7 Position your resources where they'll have the greatest impact.

8 Modern Government Procurement and Payment policies have greatly improved. Understand that the historical barriers preventing many SMBs from bidding for government business are no longer what they once were.

9 Never forget Rule number one.

GLOSSARY OF ABBREVIATIONS

SMB — Small to Medium Business
B2B — Business to Business
BAU — Business as Usual
DMs — Decision Makers
EOI — Expression of Interest
RFQ — Request for Quote
RFP — Request for Proposal
SOA — Standing Offer Arrangement
PO — Purchase Order

ACKNOWLEDGEMENTS

Throughout the adventure of writing this book, there are a few people I'd like to thank:

- My beautiful wife and kids. I am so lucky to have you all by my side for this journey. Life's great knowing we'll share many more adventures in the future.
- My patient government friends.
- My extremely patient editor Martin Rusis.
- My book designer and typesetter Helen Christie.
- My A-Team who have given me as much as I've given them over many years — watch out for them in future: Simon, Cam, Gareth, Rupesh, Muheeb, Gary, Joel, Emma, Steve, Patrick, Alice, Itvinder, Ben, Kevin, Trish, Beau, Tunny and my wood-working brother-in-arms, James. No doubt I've missed someone or two!
- John. You're a legend. Thanks.